THE
FOREST

SECOND EDITION

EARL GLISSON

Second Edition

Copyright © 2016 & 2021 by Anchor Faith Church

2121 US Hwy 1 South, Suite 28

St. Augustine, Florida 32086

Published by Anchor Faith Library

2121 US HWY 1 S, Suite 28

St. Augustine, Florida 32086

ISBN - 978-1-304-33342-1

Imprint: Lulu.com

To my loving wife, Marci.

Your commitment and faithfulness to the purpose that God has called us to is truly amazing. You constantly encouraged me to write, believing there were books inside of me needing to come out. I am grateful for your unwavering support.

Thank you for everything.

I love you.

TABLE OF CONTENTS

THE FOREST AND THE TREES

AN INTRODUCTION

Most of us have heard the expression that someone "can't see the forest for the trees." Of course, this is just an abstract way to suggest that the person in question appears to be suffering from short sightedness by focusing on certain details while missing out on the bigger picture. I wonder; have you ever considered how this saying can apply to some people's perception of the *Word of God*? At the risk of sounding cliché-ish, please allow me to submit to you that the *Bible*—in its entirety—is like a "forest" composed of many, many individual "trees." In this case, think of the "forest" as representing the overall setting, or context, of the *Bible*, with the "trees" standing for the numerous subjects and teachings found within *God's Word*. Sometimes people fixate on certain "trees," while failing to take into proper perspective the entire "forest" in which those "trees" are found. This is like wearing spiritual blinders, because we need the full view of *God's Word* to clearly understand and properly apply the bountiful truths found within it. Simply stated, as we prayerfully study the *Word of God*, we must never lose sight of its full context—so we can rightly discern and apply the *Whole Truth*.

I am reminded of a popular folktale set in a small village in India. It tells a story about six blind men who had never encountered an elephant. Then, one day, someone brought a bull pachyderm into their village, attracting a lot of attention. Filled with curiosity, these blind men sought to discover for themselves what this intriguing creature was by coming close so they could touch it. Each of them timidly approached the beast and began to skillfully use his hands and fingers to examine only part of the elephant, failing to recognize that there was more. One felt its long trunk. Another examined its smooth tusks. Another explored a floppy ear. Another ran his hands across the broad side of the beast. Another explored just a leg. The last in the group only felt the tail. As might have been expected, each of the blind men ended up with a completely different concept of an elephant. Afterwards, when they shared what they had learned with nearby onlookers, each of the men was certain that his depiction of an elephant was correct. However, they predictably all got it wrong. Regardless of their personal sincerity in sharing what they had discovered, each of the blind men's presumptions about what this interesting creature actually was lacked integrity. Not one of them got it right. Not even close. Due to failure to examine the subject fully, they missed the bigger picture. In this same manner, a skewed perspective can cause people to fail to grasp the complete picture when examining *God's Word*. As a result, sadly, they are prone to develop or to connect themselves with entire doctrines and belief systems that neglect to take into account the true overall concept and integrity of the *Bible*. This is why, as we explore the *Scriptures* to increase our understanding, we must never lose sight of the full context of the *Word of God*—from beginning to end.

Doctrines and belief systems that cause people to "fail to see the forest for the trees" are based, at best, on partial truths—often called "half truths." Take "Salvation from Sin," for instance. This is a major subject of Christian teaching, as it absolutely should be. Salvation is one truth clearly expressed in *John 3:16: "For God so loved the world, that He gave His only begotten Son, that whoever believes in Him shall not perish, but have eternal life."* Indeed, as a born-again believer and pastor who preaches the salvation message, I wholeheartedly embrace the importance of the evangelical teaching about salvation from sin. The gift of salvation made available by the grace of God for all humanity through Jesus Christ, the Son of God, with His death, burial, and resurrection, is nothing less than amazing! It is a critical truth which everyone needs to hear. However, as crucial and precious as the "Salvation from Sin" message proves to be for all who receive Christ as their Savior, we can agree that this is not the only subject of great importance in the *Bible*. Salvation opens the door to many other essential truths that God intends for us to learn. However, many churches focus so heavily on evangelism and the need to reach the lost that they fail to devote a great deal of attention to much else from *God's Word*. In fact, I have even heard pastors make comments like "Salvation is really the only thing that matters" or "Getting people saved is God's only concern." The problem is that such limited focus neglects so many other teachings from the *Word of God*, including crucial truths to which born-again Christians need to be exposed in order to grow strong in Christ.

After having received Christ as their Lord and Savior, new believers need to be nourished in the Word, so that they can grow strong in the faith, learning important teachings in the full context of the *Bible*. In this way, as they grow more mature through full exposure to *God's Word*—staying focused on the full context of the *Bible*—they will discover their God-given purpose and learn how to fulfill the Lord's divine plan for their lives. Of course, it is not just new believers who need to be nourished daily in the Word in its full context. For our faith to be strong and for us to grow mature in Christ, all believers need a steady diet of *God's Word*. *Romans 10:17* teaches, *"So then faith comes by hearing, and hearing by the Word of God."* In *1 Corinthians 3* the Apostle Paul talks about how we as believers need more than the "milk" of the word if we are to grow mature in Christ. This indicates that basic teachings are insufficient for us to grow in our faith.

As we grow in Christ, it is of paramount importance that we keep at the forefront of our vision the overall context of the *Bible*. We must never lose sight of "the forest." We can make sure of this—when we seek to gain understanding through revelation by reading and prayerfully studying particular passages from the *Holy Scriptures*—by striving to find clarity about how what we are studying fits the context of the entire *Bible*. When we delve into the *Scriptures*, it is imperative that we avoid "cherry picking" certain passages out of context with the rest. This means that we must take pains to carefully apply what we glean from studying a particular passage of scripture to the context of the testament in which it is found (*Old or New Testament*), along with the context of the book, the chapter, and all the verses in which the passage is embedded—relating all of this to the context of the *Bible* as a whole. As a rule of thumb, careful interpretation of

God's Word requires that any apparent truth that we perceive from studying a passage of scripture must be confirmed by at least two or three relevant passages found elsewhere in the *Word*. I like to refer to these supporting passages as "witnessing *Scriptures*." It cannot be overstated how important it is to be deliberate about being careful to determine how what we perceive from our comparative study fits within the context of the entire *Bible*. This way we will never lose sight of the "forest" when looking at the "trees." Only when we begin to have a full view of the "forest," will we develop a proper perspective of the "trees."

GOD THE CREATOR

All over the planet today, millions of unfulfilled individuals are looking for answers. As they search for real purpose for their lives, they often contemplate the "true meaning" of existence—as if it were a great mystery. Numerous false religions and philosophies of men have been formed, all having failed in their attempts to supply answers to help fill the void. The truth is that neither the philosophies of man nor empty religious practices can add real meaning to life.

We must be careful where and to whom we look to for learning. The *Bible* warns us to beware of false prophets and teachers who mislead people with unsound doctrines and teachings. In *Matthew 7:15 (NKJV)*, Jesus declares,

> *"Beware of false prophets, who come to you in sheep's clothing, but inwardly they are ravenous wolves."*

In *Colossians 2:8 (NKJV)*, the Apostle Paul cautions,

> *"Beware lest anyone cheat you through philosophy and empty deceit, according to the tradition of men, according to the basic principles of the world, and not according to Christ."*

Sadly, masses of people from all walks of life, from all across the earth, have been—and still are being—led astray in search of their true destiny, while the answers they seek have been available in *God's Word* all along!

Only the inspired *Word of God*, understood in its full context, "the forest," fully seen without blinders, reveals the true meaning of life! That is the one place where you can go to find the answer for why we are here in the first place—the answer that so many people are seeking to find. In fact, when the full context of the *Scriptures* becomes the framework of our everyday lives, only then can we live with true purpose. This comes when we have a full view of the "forest."

The entire *Bible* makes more sense when we gain an understanding of God's purpose for creation in the first place. To fully grasp the binding message that sets the context of *God's Word*, we must start from the beginning. *Genesis 1:1* tells us, *"In the beginning, God created the heavens and the earth."* From this opening statement, we know that it was God who created everything. But why? What was His purpose? *Psalms 90:2*, says, *"Before the mountains were born* the **earth** was **made** **for** the purpose of **being** **inhabited** *or You gave birth to the earth and the world, Even from everlasting to everlasting, You are God."* It seems incomprehensible, yet God existed before creation, itself. The *Bible* tells us who God is, how He cares about His creation, and how He feels about us.

Genesis Chapter 1 describes how creation took place over a six-day period. At the end of the third day, and at the end of each day following, God surveys the results of what He has "spoken" into existence and says that He is "pleased." He pronounces, "It is good." After evaluating His entire creation at the end of the sixth day, He proclaims, "It is very good."

God clearly valued all that He created; however, He had special regard for the human being that He created in His own image. According to the Word, God—our "Creator"—loves us! His very nature is the purest form of love. We know that it is the nature of love to always desire to give and share of itself. *John 3:16* proclaims, *"For God so loved the world that He gave His only son ..."* Therefore, we must realize that God not only knows about love; actually, according to *1 John 4:16, "God is love."* So, it makes sense that, since God is love, itself, His very nature is to give, to share, and to bestow love upon another. This is why He created the earth and placed humanity in it in the first place. He did so, in His infinite wisdom, in order that He would have a favored being to be the recipient of His affection and to enjoy a close, loving relationship with Him. This would please Him.

We know that *Isaiah 45:18* states,

> *"For thus says the Lord, who created the heavens (He is the God who formed the earth and made it, He established it and did not create it a waste place, but formed it to be inhabited)."*

According to this verse, the earth was made for the purpose of being inhabited. So, evidently, God intended for someone to live here, on earth, someone with whom He could enjoy having a personal relationship—someone whom He ultimately could endear as the very object of His great Love!

God definitely cares about his creation, and we know that He has an unwavering interest in it. The earth, which He owns by virtue of having created it, is special to Him. *Psalm 24:1* clearly states,

> *"The earth is the Lord's, and all it contains, the world, and those who dwell in it."*

So, the *Bible* says that God made this planet; it was birthed by Him, according to His own design.

If God owns the world, because He created it, then we can conclude that He retains all authority over it. From the moment that He spoke the earth into existence, He had full dominion over His creation. In fact, up until the sixth day of creation, the whole earth belonged to God—and to Him alone. Then, came the entrance of His most prized creation—the very object of His affection—humankind. In essence, the introduction of man and woman on the planet was God's crowning creation, His greatest work! And He created humankind for a purpose. Hallelujah!

THE CREATION OF MAN

Genesis 1:26-28 says, *"Then God said, 'Let us make man [humankind] in our image, according to Our likeness; and let them rule over the fish of the sea and over the birds of the sky and over the cattle, and over all the earth and over everything that creeps upon the earth.' God created man in His own image, in the image of God He created him; male and female He created them. God blessed them; and God said to them, 'Be fruitful and multiply, and fill the earth, and subdue it; and rule over the fish of the sea and over the birds of the sky and over every living thing that moves on the earth.'"*

When reading the early chapters of Genesis, the first book of the *Bible*, as we progress through the days of creation, we see the phrase: *"God spoke;"* then, we learn that whatever was "spoken" immediately happened—according to His command. Then, again, *"God spoke,"* and what He said happened; then, again, *"God spoke,"* and it happened—repeatedly, all the way from day one through day five. We see that God was able to *"speak"* things into existence. However, on the sixth day, according to *Genesis 2:7*, God did not *"speak"* man into existence. Rather, He *"formed"* man from the *"dust of the ground"* and *"breathed"* into his nostrils *"the breath of life,"* and man became a living being created in *"God's own image."* The contrast between *"God spoke"* and *"God formed"* distinctly differentiates between the manner in which plants and animals were created and the hands-on, personal attention God gave when creating man. As mentioned earlier, the first man, Adam, was God's most cherished accomplishment, His crowning achievement. Just think of it. God took His time to form man, up close and personal. Then, He intimately breathed *"the breath of life"* into His prized created being. Wow! What a great picture of God's love and care for His special created being! With this in mind, consider how the Creator of the universe has that same special, personal interest, at this very moment, in you and me! Now, that is something to really ponder. Hallelujah!

Think about it. Adam was made in God's own image and likeness. He looked like God, acted like God, and likely even talked like God. In *Luke 3:38*, Adam is even referred to as a *"son of God."* Adam was not *"God in the flesh"* like Jesus was when He walked on earth. Jesus, Who, on earth, was God wrapped in flesh, came as "the only begotten" Son of God, the Offspring of God, *"conceived by the Spirit"* and *"born of a virgin."* However, Adam was, in fact, a "created" child of God. Hence he had *"sonship"* with the Heavenly Father Who created and breathed life into him. That is why Luke called Adam "*a son of God*," not "*the Son of God*."

> Genesis 2:16-17 reads, "The Lord God commanded the man,
> saying, 'Of any tree of the garden you may eat freely, but from
> the tree of knowledge of good and evil you shall not eat, for in
> the day you eat it you shall surely die.'"

Numerous trees from which Adam could eat had been provided, with only one bearing forbidden fruit of which he had been warned by God not to partake. This tells us that there were more opportunities for Adam to live righteously than unrighteously, which is still true for us today. God gave this warning to Adam to protect and to preserve him, along with the garden which he had been given, not to deprive him of something good. It was for his protection and well being that he was to abstain from the fruit of that tree! It also afforded Adam a way to demonstrate his love for His Father by honoring Him through simple obedience. In effect, by giving Adam a choice whether or not to eat the forbidden fruit, God provided Adam a way to exercise his freedom to choose his own destiny.

In the second chapter of Genesis, we learn that, after making man, God created woman, who was called Eve, as Adam's "*helpmate*." *Genesis 2:18 (NKJV)* reads,

> "And the Lord God said, 'It is not good that man should be
> alone. I will make him a helper comparable to him.' "

Verses 21-22 tell how the Creator formed Eve from a rib taken from Adam's side, from the same substance used to make man. At this point, let us look at everything that God has given Adam. He enjoys a personal relationship with his Creator who frequents the garden. He

God gave man dominion over everything that He had created

has been placed in complete authority. And, he has been provided a *"helpmate"* personally handcrafted for him by God! How wonderful so far this must be for both of them, man and wife, having been given dominion over all things on the earth—while sharing a worry-free life in the garden! Keep in mind that there is no sin at this time. I heard one minister state it like this, "It was God, Adam, and Eve in the garden, and no sin." The earth, everything in it, and even man, himself, are all perfect. There is no sickness. No death. No sadness. No anxiety. No pain of any kind. Again, the *Scriptures* tell us how, while looking at all that He had created, *"God saw that it was very good."* So, Adam and Eve up until now are able to thrive in a perfect, sinless environment provided for them.

God not only created Adam and Eve as responsive beings with whom He could have a loving relationship, He also gave them a purpose to accomplish. *Genesis 1:26 (NLT)* states it clearly:

> *"Then God said, 'Let us make human beings in our image, to be like us. They will reign over the fish in the sea, the birds in the sky and over the cattle, and over all the earth and over everything that creeps upon the earth.'"*

The *King James Version* of this verse reads, *"...let them have dominion..."* Adam and Eve were put in the position to "rule" and to "reign" over the planet with authority bestowed upon them by their Creator. So, it is clear that **dominion was humankind's God-appointed purpose on the earth**. Adam was created as a son, then given an assignment by his Heavenly Father. *Psalm 115:16 (NIV)* reads,

> *"The highest heavens belong to the Lord, but the earth He has given to man."*

It was the delegated authority—**the dominion that God gave him as a son—which enabled Adam, along with his wife, to rule over the planet for God.**

THE FALL OF MAN

In *Genesis Chapter 3*, we learn how Adam made a tragic decision with far-reaching consequences. Many people know this account merely as a religious story about "the forbidden fruit and the banishment of Adam and Eve from the Garden." However, the record of what happened on that eventful day in the Garden of Eden is much more profound than mere banishment from the garden. We need to take into account all that was lost to humankind when Adam disobeyed God. This tragic loss reveals a far-reaching price that was paid through "the fall of humankind by giving away dominion." Let me repeat. Adam and Eve did not just suffer banishment from the garden; they stepped down from their righteous position of dominion. Actually, what transpired long ago in the Garden of Eden—when dominion was relinquished—explains the nagging, empty feeling inside of so many people who lack **true** purpose for their lives today. What was given away in the Garden of Eden was God's appointed purpose for our lives. Our Creator still has the very same purpose for us today, and—as we shall see as we explore "the forest"—He has provided a Way for us to recover and embrace His purpose for our lives!

In *Genesis 3:1-7*, we read,

> *"Now the serpent was craftier than any beast of the field which the Lord God had made. And he said to the woman, 'Indeed, has God said, "You shall not eat from any tree of the garden?"' The woman said to the serpent, "From the fruit of the trees of the garden we may eat; but from the fruit of the tree which is in the middle of the garden, God has said, 'You shall not eat from it or touch it, or you will die.'" The serpent said to the woman, 'You surely will not die! For God knows that in the day you eat from it your eyes will be opened, and you will be like God, knowing good and evil.' When the woman saw that the tree was good for food, and that it was a delight to the eyes, and that the tree was desirable to make one wise, she took from its fruit and ate; and she gave also to her husband with her, and he ate. Then the eyes of both of them were opened, and they knew that they were naked; and they sewed fig leaves together and made themselves loin coverings."*

From these verses, we see how the serpent approaches Eve

with the intent of deceiving her. He successfully convinces her that she will find it advantageous to partake of the fruit from the *"tree of knowledge of good and evil."* So, Eve does as the serpent suggests, and subsequently she turns to her husband, Adam, offering him the fruit to eat, which he amazingly does! Seriously? With full knowledge of the command and forewarning of the Lord, Who unfailingly has been the perfect Father—and with awareness that God made him the first person to whom dominion was given as a sacred gift—Adam still foolishly chooses to ignore his Father's warning? He willfully disobeys? At that point, by ignoring and disobeying God, Adam exercises his own free will; by committing this sin, he knowingly gives away his God-given authority and dominion over the earth to the usurper—the enemy. By giving in to temptation, He chooses to step down from his position of authority and dominion in which God has placed him, choosing a different direction than appointed by God. He loses his good standing with his Father and is no longer qualified to fulfill his God-appointed purpose. And nothing else can ever fill this gap.

We know that Adam handed over to the enemy what God had given him, because Satan later tells Jesus in *Luke 4:6*, "... *I will give you all this domain and its glory; for it has been handed over to me* ..." Satan says this in specific reference to Adam's treason against God. Adam could have rejected Eve's offer of the fruit and, thereby, would have retained his position of authority and dominion. Instead, he consciously decided to give up his God-given purpose on the earth, choosing to rebel against the will of his Heavenly Father. In effect, he elected to turn over his position of authority and dominion to the usurper, Satan. As a result of Adam's willful and reckless action, Satan legally gains dominion over the earth. This is the key point. By choosing to sin, Adam steps down from and vacates his proper position of dominion over the earth, losing his good standing. He literally walks away from his God-appointed purpose and from his personal relationship with his Heavenly Father.

We also know that—when Adam chose to relinquish his position of dominion over the earth—sin entered into human nature, and humanity immediately became separated from God, falling out of good standing with His Kingdom government. In essence, at this point, God's original plan seemed to have failed, but the *Bible* tells us of the Creator's plans to ultimately provide another Way to fulfill His original intent in and on this earth.

As mentioned earlier, most people today—believers and non-believers alike—are at least somewhat familiar with the account of what happened in the Garden of Eden. They have some understanding about "the fall of humankind." However, let me emphasize again that, unfortunately, many fail to grasp the full significance of what took place. The loss of dominion put Adam in a position in which he was never designed to be, and it gave the enemy, Satan, a position he should never have occupied. Through Adam's disobedience to God, Satan was able to ursurp the authority and dominion over this earth for himself, and humankind no longer held the rightful authority to reign over creation.

Dominion is the power to rule and to reign, and Adam handed dominion, in and on the earth, to the enemy. As previously stated, Adam fell from his place of God-given authority to rule and to reign and, through his disobedience, he also lost his personal relationship with God. The earth at this point entered into its "fallen state," evident in the *Bible* from *Genesis 3* all the way through *Revelation 20*. Most preachers and churches today focus almost entirely on these chapters of the *Bible* and concentrate on the "Fallen State of Humanity," but this is not the full context of *God's Word*. You have to increase your view to see "the forest."

if **adam** had **never** **eaten** the fruit **where** would adam be **today?**

We must recognize that what happened in the garden was not about Adam losing a spot in Heaven, because, before he sinned, he was not waiting to go to Heaven in the first place. Heaven was never the prize after which Adam was seeking, because—prior to the fall— Adam and Eve were already living eternally in the Garden of Eden—where Heaven appeared on earth. It was, after all, where God walked daily. So, for us to "see the forest for the trees," I ask that you consider what humanity would be doing if there had never been any sin in the earth. We need to examine God's original intent for this planet. In so doing, we will gain an immense understanding of *His Word* and of His purpose for us all. First, this requires that we willingly set aside preconceived ideas and notions we may have about Jesus, about the *Holy Scriptures*, and about the Kingdom of God, in order to re-examine and test—against the full context of the *Bible*—all that we think we know about religion and much of what we have heard about Christianity. Then, seeking to have our minds renewed through the full context of *God's Word*, being guided by the Holy Spirit, we will be prepared to open our eyes to see fully Who our Creator is, what it is like to have a right relationship with Him, and what His plans are for us as we go about our lives.

For us to be able to see the "forest" fully, we must be careful not to allow religious ideology or even traditional thinking to blur our vision. In *Matthew 15:3 (NKJV)*, Jesus asks,

> " ... *Why do you also transgress the commandment of God because of your tradition?*"

To "see the forest," we must first clear out all of the clutter, so to speak, so that our minds, under the guidance of the Holy Spirit, can be "renewed" by the *Whole Truth* of the *Word of God*. *Romans 12:2* instructs us, " ... *be transformed by the renewing of the mind ...*"

Now, I am not asking you to believe my opinions or some new doctrine; rather, I only challenge you to let the *Word of God* define itself. As we seek to fulfill our hunger to know God's truth, we must never decide in advance what we, personally, hold to be true, and then go searching through the *Scriptures* to find support for our predetermined conclusions. The surest approach to discerning truth is to place ourselves under the guidance of the Holy Spirit, who, as Jesus promised, will "teach" us (see *John 14:26*). When we allow the *Scriptures*, themselves, under the guidance of the Holy Spirit, to form and dictate our beliefs, we will never be misled. God is well able to speak for Himself through *His Word*. By shaking off anything that would interfere with our ability to receive from Him, which can include preconceived thinking, we will be able to improve our view of the "forest" through the "trees."

I would like for you to understand that this *Bible*, this so-called "religious book," is actually not really about religion, nor is it about a particular religion or religions. Not at all. Actually, the *Bible* is about the King, His Kingdom, and His royal offspring! That is the correct context of the *Bible*. God's purpose is for us to become citizens of His Kingdom, to stay in good standing with His government, and to enjoy a personal relationship with the King! **The "forest" of the *Bible* is, in fact, the Kingdom of God!**

Every truth within the *Bible* should be viewed and understood through the lens of God's Kingdom. The Kingdom was, from the beginning, and still is, His purpose and plan for creation. Glory to God! I get really excited just thinking about how all of us who choose to make Jesus our Lord become citizens of His Kingdom and how we are afforded the privilege of advancing that Kingdom to the ends of the earth!!! Now, you might say, "Pastor, I don't see God's Kingdom.

Where is it?" Not to worry; in later chapters, we will further explore what the *Bible* says about the Kingdom.

Meanwhile, do you ever ask yourself, "What if Adam had never eaten the fruit? Where would he be today?" I have heard many answers when asking for responses to these questions from the pulpit over the years. Some have volunteered that Adam would "still be enjoying life in the Garden of Eden." Others have responded that he would "still be in God's presence." Some have said that he would "still be ruling over creation." All of these answers, while correct, go beyond the simple answer I was seeking—that he would "still be on the earth today, where God intended for him to live forever!" In other words, there would be no waiting to get to Heaven. We must recognize that, before "the fall," Adam was not trying to get to Heaven to live with God in another realm. As we mentioned earlier, God actually often visited Him on earth in the Garden of Eden. Adam enjoyed all the provision he would ever need, without having to worry about a single thing. God originally intended for Adam and his helpmate, Eve, to stay forever in the "garden of plenty" and to continue to exercise dominion over the earth. So, as part of being able to "see the forest for the trees," let us consider what humanity would be doing if there had never been any sin in the earth.

You see, we know that Heaven existed even before God created the universe and all the things in it. God still rules from there—supreme in authority. Heaven is not a product of our imagination. It is very real, although it exists in the "unseen" spiritual realm—for "God is Spirit." Jesus taught, "For God is Spirit, so those who worship him must worship in spirit and in truth" *John 4:24 (NLT).* In *2 Corinthians 4:18*, spiritual things are described like this:

"... while we look, not at the things which are seen, but at the

things which are not seen; for the things which are seen are
temporal, but the things which are not seen are eternal."

In this "unseen" Heavenly realm, God rules as King over everything. In no part of Heaven does His will go unperformed or underperformed. However, another realm also exists, because the Heavenly King decided to create a "seen realm" evident here—in and around the planet earth which we occupy. From the beginning, God's desire was, and it still is, to expand His Heavenly Kingdom to this created world. Since this physical realm where we live is tangible to our natural senses, God provided a tangible way to expand His Kingdom from the "unseen realm" into the created "seen realm." Here is where humankind's real purpose is to be realized, **in advancing the Kingdom of God—in and on the earth**. God created humankind so that—through us, His created beings formed in His likeness—He could fill the earth with His Heavenly Kingdom. That is why Adam existed in the first place. That is what he would still be doing today, if he had abstained from partaking of the forbidden fruit. Adam would still be enjoying his full Kingdom authority and dominion over all the earth today, if he had simply chosen to obey his Creator.

WHAT IS A KINGDOM?

—————————————————

CHAPTER FOUR

Remember how we said that the "forest" of the *Bible*, the full context of *God's Word* that ties the rest of the *Word* together, is the "Kingdom?" Before moving further along, I think it is best to define exactly what a kingdom is, along with what it is not. By gaining a better understanding of the term, we can more clearly understand the *Word of God* in its proper context. A kingdom certainly is neither a religion nor a philosophy. Rather, a kingdom is a form of government based upon a concept of legalities. Now, we are not referring to "legalism" (i.e., dependence on law over personal faith) when we talk about

God's Kingdom, but there are legally binding laws put in place by our Creator as part of His government. In God's Kingdom, everything that the Heavenly King proclaims is, in essence, a law meant to be willingly obeyed without exception. It should be our heart's desire to obey our King to please Him, to remain submissive to His will.

By definition, in a kingdom, the king—who reigns supreme in authority—rules with absolute authority over his territory and over all who reside therein. The king's word is absolute! When he issues a decree, what he says is final! There are no decisions made by a majority vote. Citizens of a kingdom are neither afforded the liberty to create laws which they like nor do they have the power to abolish laws which they find disagreeable. The king, himself, is neither elected nor demoted by the people, because a king becomes the rightful ruler solely by virtue of birthright. A kingdom is not a democracy; rather, it is a form of government which influences the citizens through the king's personal will, intent, and purpose.

Think about it. Right now, in the unseen *"spirit realm,"* there exists a government known as the "Kingdom of God." It is the same Kingdom about which Jesus spoke in *John 3:3,*

> *"Most assuredly, I say to you, unless one is born again, he cannot see the Kingdom of God."*

This Kingdom is where God sits on His spiritual throne as the ruling authority of His government. As we shall see later in the *Scriptures,* from His throne, God has decreed that His royal "reborn" children, empowered by His Spirit, spread this unseen Kingdom into the visible "physical realm" here—in and on the earth!

Now, you might say, "Pastor. I don't see God's kingdom." Not to worry. Let me explain. Since we have established that the Kingdom of God is a government, we must first define what a government is.

Generally speaking, we think of government as a system by which a state or community is ruled. Typically, it consists of a collective, a group of persons with executive authority to exercise power and to delegate. The governmental body creates and sets into motion policies and laws. Through these means, a state's or principality's laws and policies, as well as its mechanisms for determining, implementing, and carrying out policies, are created, upheld, and enforced. Some examples of earthly governments include democracies, theocracies, communist states, socialist states, dictatorships, and monarchies, to name but a few. These forms of government represent ideologies which exist within the minds of humans as abstract thoughts, in essence, in the "unseen realm." Those ideologies are made manifest by agents and agencies in the "physical realm." Just as these governments are real, existing on the planet today, so does the Kingdom of God exist in the "unseen spiritual realm." His royal government is made manifest through the lives of His agents here on earth—those people who submit to His supreme authority as their King—as citizens of His Kingdom. Jesus, himself, said in *Luke 17:21*,

> " ... *nor will they say, 'Look, here it is!' or, 'There it is!' For behold, the Kingdom of God is in your midst."*

Therefore, the existence of God's Kingdom—which is a spiritual Kingdom not evident to everyone, at least for now—must be "revealed" in the lives and lifestyles of its citizens who love and obey their Heavenly King.

I personally believe that the very concept of a kingdom is actually something birthed by God, Himself, and placed by Him inside the human heart. It is the oldest form of government on the earth and also the most recognized. Kingdoms are frequently depicted in movies, on television, and in books. I mean ... think about it for a moment.

a **kingdom** is not a **democracy** but rather is a form of government that influences the citizens through the **king's** personal **will**, **purpose**, and **intent**

Have you ever considered why the setting for so many popular stories and fairytales is an imaginary kingdom someplace? The very notion of a kingdom stimulates the innermost parts of humanity. Perhaps this is because, deep down in the human spirit, there is a yearning to be part of God's Kingdom. Actually, as far as I can see, there is no doubt about that!

We must realize that the Kingdom of God, also called the "Kingdom of Heaven," is ordained by God. It encompasses everything within His reign and rule. The root of the word "kingdom" means "king's domain," referring to all over which the king retains dominion or authoritative control. For now, God's Kingdom, in the "spirit realm," rules over those of us who are fully submitted to His will. However, there will come a time when God's Kingdom will rule over the planet in its entirety. *Revelation 21:5* says,

> *"And He who sits on the throne said: 'Behold, I am making all things new.' And He said, "Write, for these words are faithful and true."*

And *Revelation 5:10 (NIV)* proclaims,

> *"You have made them to be a kingdom and priests to serve our God, and they will reign on the earth."*

Much like the first two chapters of the *Bible*, the last two chapters of *God's Word* show the earth once again in its perfect state. For a full description, I invite you to take a close look at *Revelation 21 and 22*, where you will find *Scriptures* that reveal how the Kingdom of God will one day physically manifest itself on this planet, where the citizens of His Kingdom will rule and reign with King Jesus forever! These final two chapters of the *Bible* describe how Jesus Christ will rule and reign on a "new earth" as the "King of kings" and "Lord of lords." At that time, God's Heavenly Kingdom will be tangible to our natural senses once again, just as He intended at the beginning of creation. This is His plan! Hallelujah!

THE SERPENT

As we increase our understanding about God's Kingdom, it is important to fully identify the serpent who appears in the Garden of Eden, in *Genesis Chapter 3*, and to uncover the true motives behind his actions. Too often, people glance over the passages that describe what transpired on that critical day in the Garden, taking note of the serpent's deceptive actions as the "tempter" of Eve, while overlooking his deeply moted intentions. We know from the *Scriptures* that the serpent's real identity, as previously stated, is the devil, whose name is Satan. He is also called "the enemy." Jesus said, as quoted in *Luke*

10:18, "And He said to them, 'I was watching Satan fall from heaven like lightning.'" Satan was cast down from Heaven to the earth. Though he once existed in Heaven with God, he was banished and exiled. But why? To gain more understanding, let us examine both *Isaiah 14* and *Ezekiel 28*:

> *Isaiah 14:12-19:* "*How you have fallen from heaven, O star of the morning, son of the dawn! You have been cut down to the earth, You who have weakened the nations! But you said in your heart, 'I will ascend to heaven; I will raise my throne above the stars of God, And I will sit on the mount of assembly In the recesses of the north. I will ascend above the heights of the clouds; I will make myself like the Most High.' Nevertheless you will be thrust down to Sheol, To the recesses of the pit. Those who see you will gaze at you, They will ponder over you, saying, 'Is this the man who made the earth tremble, Who shook kingdoms, Who made the world like a wilderness And overthrew its cities, Who did not allow his prisoners to go home?' All the kings of the nations lie in glory, Each in his own tomb. But you have been cast out of your tomb Like a rejected branch, Clothed with the slain who are pierced with a sword, Who go down to the stones of the pit Like a trampled corpse.*"

> *Ezekiel 28:11-17:* "*Again the word of the Lord came to me saying, 'Son of man, take up a lamentation over the king of Tyre and say to him, "Thus says the Lord God, 'You had the seal of perfection, Full of wisdom and perfect in beauty. You were in Eden, the garden of God; Every precious stone was your covering: The ruby, the topaz and the diamond;*

Adam gave the **rulership** of the planet over to the devil when he **disobeyed** God.

The beryl, the onyx and the jasper; The lapis lazuli, the turquoise and the emerald; And the gold, the workmanship of your settings and sockets, Was in you. On the day that you were created They were prepared. You were the anointed cherub who covers, And I placed you there. You were on the holy mountain of God; You walked in the midst of the stones of fire. You were blameless in your ways From the day you were created Until unrighteousness was found in you. By the abundance of your trade You were internally filled with violence, And you sinned; Therefore I have cast you as profane From the mountain of God. And I have destroyed you, O covering cherub, From the midst of the stones of fire. Your heart was lifted up because of your beauty; You corrupted your wisdom by reason of your splendor. I cast you to the ground; I put you before kings, That they may see you.'"

It is clearly shown, in *Isaiah 14:13*, that Satan wanted to lead a rebellion to usurp God's Kingdom. Because of his pride, Satan refused to worship and to bow down to his Creator, and he wanted to "raise a throne of his own" above God's. In essence, the created being wanted to rule his Creator. It was his will to instigate rebellion against God's Heavenly Kingdom. He longed to take authority over God's government. This was his deepest desire, his primary motivation. We read, in *Ezekiel 28:15*, that *"unrighteousness"* had been found in Satan. That was the reason he was cast out of Heaven. Now, the word "righteous" means "right standing," or "upstanding," so the term "unrighteousness" is used to describe Satan's having fallen out of "good standing" with God's governing authority. We know that Satan lost his "right standing" with the governing authority, and he was thereby permanently exiled from God's Kingdom. *Revelation 12:9* says, " ... *he [Satan] was cast to earth, and his angels were cast out with him.*"

When Satan observed Adam in the garden, it stands to reason that he would have thought, "He looks a lot like God." Undoubtedly, he would have felt jealous, because Adam had been made in God's image and had been given the position and authority to exercise dominion. Satan likely would have pondered, "Although God wouldn't bow down to me, perhaps this man who looks like Him would do so." In essence, it would be another prideful and rebellious attempt to exalt himself to the place of God. Here stood the humans who, with authority given to them by God, ruled over this world. They were in "right standing" in God's Kingdom, while he, himself, had been exiled as "unrighteous." Satan would have pondered, "What can I do to change their position? How can I trick them into losing their right standing?" He saw his opportunity to usurp Adam's dominion authority and to exalt himself into a ruling position like God.

Sadly, by electing to ignore God's warning to never partake of the forbidden fruit, Adam allowed Satan to accomplish his purpose. By disobeying his Heavenly Father, Adam vacated his position of dominion, thereby handing it over to the enemy. As a result, Satan became, as Jesus referred to him, in *John 16:11*, "*... the ruler of this world.*" Adam foolishly turned the rulership of the planet over to the devil. In other words, Satan became the king of this world's system, although, as we will discuss in the next chapter, that would not last forever. By willfully choosing to sin, Adam turned his dominion over to the enemy, giving up his God-given position and his righteous relationship with his Creator. Remember what we said earlier. Adam did not lose a religion; he lost personal access to the *Kingdom of God*.

Stand assured, the present ruler of the earth does not want you, me, or anyone else to know about God's Kingdom: "*In whose case the god of this world has blinded the minds of the unbelieving so that they might not see the light of the Gospel of the glory of Christ, who is the image of God"* (2 Corinthians 4:4). This shows how the enemy attempts to keep people spiritually "blind," so that they will fail to become part of the Kingdom of God and to participate in it. Jesus defeated the enemy through the cross and His resurrection, but Satan still travails to keep as many people as possible in darkness—well out of God's Kingdom—by deceiving them with empty religion and blinding falsehoods. Thank God for the Light which illuminates the only Way to enter into the Kingdom of God! Jesus Christ!

THE ROYAL SEED

The fall of humankind through Adam's disobedience was not part of God's design, nor was it His desire, nor did what happened catch Him by surprise. *Isaiah 46:10* tells us, *"Declaring the end from the beginning, And from ancient times things which have not been done, Saying, 'My purpose will be established, And I will accomplish all My good pleasure.'"* You can be sure that nothing ever catches God off guard!

Let us look at *Genesis 3:8-19*:

"Then the man and his wife heard the sound of the Lord God as he was walking in the garden in the cool of the day, and they hid from the Lord God among the trees of the garden. But the Lord God called to the man, 'Where are you?' He answered, "I heard you in the garden, and I was afraid because I was naked; so I hid." And he said, 'Who told you that you were naked? Have you eaten from the tree that I commanded you not to eat from?' The man said, "The woman you put here with me—she gave me some fruit from the tree, and I ate it." Then the Lord God said to the woman, 'What is this you have done?' The woman said, "The serpent deceived me, and I ate." So the Lord God said to the serpent, 'Because you have done this, Cursed are you above all livestock and all wild animals! You will crawl on your belly and you will eat dust all the days of your life. And I will put enmity between you and the woman, and between your offspring and hers; he will crush your head, and you will strike his heel.' To the woman he said, 'I will make your pains in childbearing very severe; with painful labor you will give birth to children. Your desire will be for your husband, and he will rule over you.' To Adam he said, 'Because you listened to your wife and ate fruit from the tree about which I commanded you, You must not eat from it, Cursed is the ground because of you; through painful toil you will eat food from it all the days of your life. It will produce thorns and thistles for you, and you will eat the plants of the field. By the sweat of your brow you will eat your food until you return to the ground, since from it you were taken; for dust you are and to dust you will return.'"

We learn from the above passage of scripture that, immediately after the fall of humanity, God calls to Adam in the garden saying, *"Where are you?"* We know that God, being omniscient, obviously is not attempting to uncover Adam's hiding place by calling out to him. Rather, God is challenging Adam to consider, "Where are you now?" In essence, He is admonishing Adam, inviting him to take a look at how his position has changed for the worse. God is confronting Adam with his treason. Notice that Adam indirectly blames God by trying to shift responsibility to his wife. *"The woman whom YOU [emphasis added] gave to be with me, she gave me from the tree, and I ate."* That is what sin nature does; it always tries to assign blame somewhere else. Sin, simply put, is disobeying God at *His Word*. Clearly, Eve has been deceived by the serpent; never-the-less, Adam must remain accountable for his own actions.

No way, whatsoever, was Adam under the deception that what he was doing was in any way permissible. When he made the choice to partake of the fruit, it was a willful and personally accountable act of rebellion against God's will, which is sin. The fact that Adam sinned meant that the very DNA of his being became infected with the sin nature. From that point on, every time humanity reproduced, the child would be born into sin. Adam opened up an epidemic of sin, now embedded in the gene pool of the human race. You could say the bloodline of humanity was altered and its royal status displaced. As things now stood, unrighteousness separated humankind from God. Because of sin, humanity lost its ability to fulfill its purpose.

After confronting Adam and Eve, God then turned to the serpent and placed him under a curse for having deceived the woman. In *Genesis 3:14*, we read, *"God said to the serpent, 'Because you have done this, Cursed are you above all livestock and all wild animals! You will crawl on your belly and you will eat dust all the days of your*

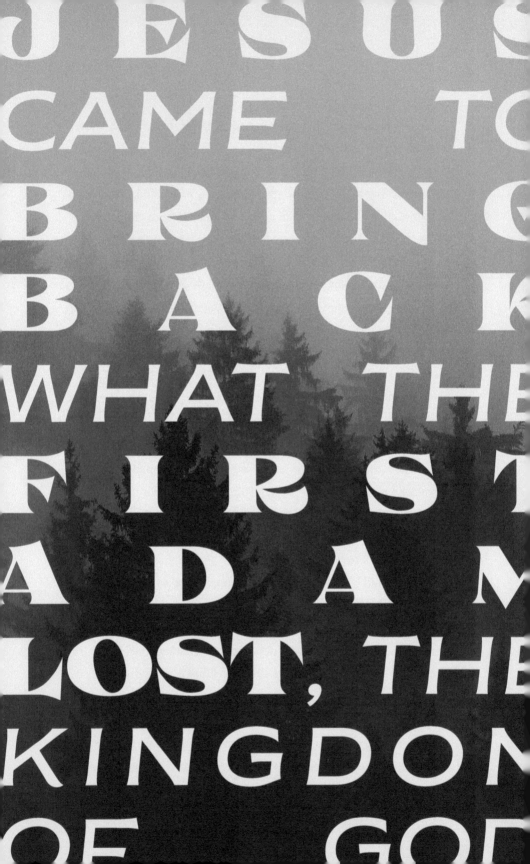

life.'" The enemy committed a crime against God and His Kingdom; therefore, he would be punished.

At this point, in His infinite wisdom, God reveals His plan for humanity's ultimate redemption. *Genesis 3:15* states,

> *"And I will put enmity between you [the serpent, Satan] and the woman, and between your offspring and hers; he will crush your head, and you will strike his heel."*

This scripture is prophetic. We know the "He" in this verse refers to the "Seed of God," Who is Jesus Christ, Who would be coming through "the woman" in order to crush the head of the serpent, Satan. As a result of one man's willful transgression, sin entered the world. For this reason, Jesus would have to enter into the world in human form through a woman, born of a virgin and conceived by the Holy Spirit.

> *Matthew 1:18 (NKJV), says, " ... she [the virgin Mary] was found with child of the Holy Spirit."*

Jesus would fulfill the prophecy spoken by His Father (see Genesis 3:15 above). The fulfillment of this prophecy is made clear in Hebrews 2:14 (NIV), which says,

> *"Since the children have flesh and blood, he [Jesus] too shared in their humanity so that by his death he might break the power of death--that is, the devil."*

Jesus would be born without sin, just as Adam was free from sin when first created. In *1 Corinthians 15:45*, Jesus is referred to as "... *the last Adam* ..." God's plan to redeem humanity was to send His only begotten Son to earth as "the last Adam" to recover for humankind what the "first Adam" relinquished. God would restore dominion, and

He would bestow upon those who would make Jesus Lord a personal relationship with the King along with the right to enter into and participate as a citizen in the Kingdom. Hallelujah!

God—through His seed, Jesus—would defeat Satan and restore all members of humanity who accept Jesus as their Lord and Savior. If you restore something, you are literally putting it back into its original position. For instance, if a book falls from the bookshelf and you retrieve it and place it on the coffee table, you have failed to restore the book—because it has not been put back in its original position. In order for something out of position to be restored, it must be put back in its original place. God sent Jesus to the earth so that humanity, having fallen from its original position of dominion because of Adam's sin, could, by individual choice, be restored into the Royal Family! Jesus, as the Son of man, took back the authority, dominion, and rule that Adam lost to Satan. Through Him, our right standing with God can be restored! Amen!

We know that God originally gave dominion over the earth to the first Adam who later forfeited his right of rulership by willfully sinning. Since God rules as King, and kingdoms operate based upon legalities, it was necessary that He use a man "born free from sin," just as Adam had been sin-free in the very beginning, to restore the dominion which Adam had relinquished to Satan as a "result of sin." In other words, to legally restore humankind's right to enter into and to participate in the Kingdom of God, the Son of God had to clothe Himself with humanity—as a "second Adam innocent of sin."

John 1:14 (NIV) says, "The Word became flesh and made his dwelling among us. We have seen his glory, the glory of the one and only Son, who came from the Father, full of grace and truth."

God never violates *His Word*, so Jesus came from the Father to the earth in the flesh as a man of unblemished righteousness—able to restore everything that the first Adam foreited. Praise God!!

GOD SEEKS A NATION

In light of being able "to see the forest," let us consider the *Old Testament* account of how God made a covenant with a people of His choosing—the Israelites—and see why that proves relevant to all of us.

In *Genesis chapter 12*, God speaks to a righteous man named Abram, "*Now the Lord said to Abram, 'Go forth from your country, And from your relatives And from your father's house, To the land which I will show you; And I will make you a great nation, And I will bless you, And make your name great; And so you shall be a blessing; And I will bless those who bless you, And the one who curses you I will curse. And in you all the families of the earth will be blessed.'"* We learn from this passage how God conveyed to Abram His far-reaching plans to make him a "great nation." It is worth noting that God did not say, "I have plans to use you to start a great religion called Judaism." Nor did He promise, "I plan to make you the father of new religions called Judaism and Christianity." Rather, God specifically promised to use Abram to make a "nation." Not a religion. A nation.

The word "nation" is not a religious term at all! It is defined by the online Oxford Dictionary as "... a large body of people united by common descent, history, culture, or language, inhabiting a particular country or territory."* After promising that He would make Abram's name "great," God renamed him "Abraham"—meaning "father of many nations." In essence, with God, everything has always been about His Kingdom—not a religion.

The *Scriptures* tell how Abraham fathered Isaac, who then begat Jacob—who eventually had his name changed to Israel. We learn that Israel formed a nation of 12 tribes that still exists on the planet today! The *Bible* affirms that the nation of Israel is God's "chosen" people. They are the particular people or "nation" that God selected for a special covenant between Himself and them.

> *In 2 Samuel 7:23 (NIV), we read, "And who is like your people Israel—the one nation on earth that God went out to redeem as a people for himself."*

As we talked about earlier, God originally created humankind to have a loving relationship with Him as part of His Kingdom. This is why He made a covenant with a chosen people. He desired to fulfill His original loving intent, so—through His chosen people—He endeavored to re-establish His Kingdom in and on the earth. Through

---

"Nation." Oxford English Dictionary. Oxford University Press, June 2021, www.oed.com. Accessed 15 June 2021.

God wanted a **covenant people** on the earth that **demonstrated** His **kingship** to the world.

His covenant with the people of Israel, He wanted to establish His Kingdom government through a separate chosen nation with Him present as the Head. Effectively, God desired to demonstrate to the rest of the world the culture of His Kingdom, as He intended to display His love and goodness in relationship with the chosen people of Israel. Essentially, the Kingdom culture would consist of the following: Worship God as King and obey Him so that He will bless you in all aspects of life. Adhere to the guidelines of the Kingdom culture and gain the benefits of the Kingdom lifestyle! The point was that God lovingly desired to have a special relationship with His covenant people on the earth, and He wanted them to love and obey Him—demonstrating the Kingdom lifestyle to the world.

Unfortunately, despite God's good intentions for them, the people of Israel often failed to obey Him. In fact, they strayed from God numerous times—which resulted in a life filled with oppression and hardship. In *Genesis 15:13*, God said to Abram, *"Know for certain that your descendants will be strangers in a land that is not theirs, where they will be enslaved and oppressed four hundred years."* This refers to the 400-year span that the Israelites would be in bondage to the Pharaoh of Egypt. However, God had a plan to free and redeem His chosen people through a man named Moses. In *Exodus 5:1*, Moses, a representative of God, informed the Pharaoh, of God's orders to *"let My people go."* God would be their King, instead of Pharaoh. It was the Most High King speaking to another kingly ruler about taking possession of His nation. God, as King, made a demand of Pharaoh, through his spokesman, Moses, to free His nation from bondage.

Upon delivering His chosen people from Egypt, God then led the Israelites into the wilderness. He subsequently gave Moses the *Ten Commandments*. These commandments—along with the rest of *The Law* handed down by Moses—provided the necessary guidelines and rules to follow in order to operate successfully in the Kingdom. By observing *The Law*, a citizen of Israel could stay in right standing with God's government and demonstrate the culture of His Kingdom to the world. *The Law* was never meant to "save" anyone, because that would require a "Savior." Although adherence to *The Law* had the power to produce the lifestyle of the Kingdom, the people's sinful nature would get in the way, making evident their need for a Savior. So God's plan for the Kingdom lifestyle to be demonstrated to the rest of the world by his chosen nation was not fully realized because of humankind's sinful nature.

Meanwhile, despite God's repeated efforts on behalf of His chosen nation, the unthinkable happened. In *1 Samuel 8:7*, God told His prophet, Samuel, *"Listen to all that the people are saying to you, they have not rejected you but they have rejected me as king."* This verse shows us that God's desire was to be King of His people. Although God desired to be the only King over Israel, the present Head of the nation, the people rejected Him and implored Samuel to find for them a man to be their earthly king. They wanted someone whom they could see and with whom they could identify. Although it displeased Him, God allowed this to take place. He knew that a nation governed by a man was not the best plan for humanity. Today, most of the world embraces the idea that "powers that be" in government can potentially fix all of society's problems, but they are only partially correct. Man-made governments will never be able to perfect society; only God's Kingdom government can do that and, ultimately, as the *Bible* foretells, it will do so.

In effect, even as He was establishing His covenant with Abram (Abraham), promising to make his name great and to make him a great nation, God was already laying the groundwork for a second covenant. There would be a "better covenant" to come that would be connected to the bloodline of Abraham. *The Law* would not redeem humankind, but there would be "the Way."

We learn in the *New Testament* about God's "new covenant" of grace and redemption through the blood of Jesus Christ, offered because of His loving desire for all people on earth to come to Him. In fact, the basis of the Apostle Paul's ministry was to proclaim the *Gospel* to the Gentile nations. In other words, the Good News of the Kingdom was meant not just for Israel but for the entire world! We know the *Bible* says, in *2 Peter 3:9,* " ... *not wishing for any to perish but for all to come to repentance."*

God will never force us to accept Him as Lord and King. It is our own choice. However, those who have accepted His Son, Jesus Christ, as their Lord and Savior, are a blessed and fulfilled people on the earth today. Jesus made a way for them to be restored into the position of dominion that Adam relinquished. They are established in His Kingdom at this very moment and entitled to enjoy all of its benefits. It is His Kingdom which will be the only one to continue to exist for eternity—in Heaven and here, in and on the earth. God has always wanted us to be part of His Kingdom! Through Christ, He has given us the keys!

OLD TESTAMENT AND THE KINGDOM

While the particular phrase "Kingdom of God" goes unmentioned in the *Old Testament*, the concept of God's Kingdom is evident throughout. *Psalm 10:16* tells us, *"The Lord is King forever and ever; Nations have perished from His land."* And *Psalm 47:7* proclaims, *"For God is the King of all the earth; Sing praises with a skillful psalm."* Even King Jehoshaphat declares, in *2 Chronicles 20:6,* *"O Lord, the God of our fathers, are You not God in the heavens? And are You not ruler over all the kingdoms of the nations? Power and might are in Your hand so that no one can stand against You."*

We see clearly in the *Old Testament* that God is declared King! In fact, that is one reason why the nation of Israel rejected Jesus when He came to earth. They were awaiting a deliverer. "The Messiah," as they referred to him, who would establish himself as an earthly king ready to take charge and to overthrow their enemies, lifting them from oppression. They envisioned this Messiah setting up a visible earthly throne from which He would govern and protect them. They missed the true Messiah, because He came as a *"suffering servant"* (*Isaiah 53*) who did not resemble the warrior king for whom they had long awaited. Jesus came first as a *"suffering servant,"* as prophesied, who would lay down His life as a sacrifice for our sins. However, it is important to realize that Jesus is no longer the "suffering servant." He finished paying our ransom and now sits at the right hand of the Father as the Almighty King Who reigns!

Many Christians today "miss the forest for the trees," by failing to view Jesus from a full Kingdom mindset. They limit their view of our Lord to His role as the Savior, focusing mainly on His having suffered on the cross and on His resurrection. Many believers misguidedly believe that they have to die and then go to Heaven to become part of His Kingdom. Well, I thank God that His Son came so that we could be saved from our sin; however, Jesus' purpose for coming was not only to save us. He endured the cross so that He could redeem us, re-establishing, in and on the earth, the Kingdom of God in which we can be active citizens—right now, rather than later! **We do not have to wait to go to Heaven to be part of His spiritual Kingdom!** He brought with Him the keys of the Kingdom! THAT is the good news! It is what the *Gospel* is all about! Jesus came to restore humanity's personal relationship with God that comes with the dominion which Adam threw away! This is received by choice. We should know and embrace our Lord, not only as our Savior, but as the "King of kings." Our reigning King who redeems and restores us to our proper place as royal citizens of His Kingdom government. He is our Lord who loves and blesses us, and He is the King of kings whom we love, emulate, willingly obey, and joyfully serve—the One with Whom we reign!

Our focus as believers should be more on Jesus the "King of kings" than the "suffering Servant." Even those inspired writers of the *Old Testament* understood this, which is why the psalmist wrote, *"For the Lord is the great God, the great King above all gods."* This is not to diminish the importance of our call to follow Christ's example of service to others, even to the point of being willing to die for others. In *Matthew 23:11*, Jesus says, *"But the greatest among you shall be your servant."* However, we should not limit our view of the "King of kings" to where we see Him only as the suffering Servant and Savior. Jesus did not come just to save us from hell. He came to invite us to rule with Him in His Kingdom! Amen!

Throughout the *Old Testament*, we see types and shadows (pictures of things to come) of Jesus coming as the Lord and Savior of man. Lord means one who is "supreme in authority," which is who King Jesus truly is; whereas, Savior refers only to what He did for us on the cross. In essence, the King, who is our Lord, interceded by laying down His life to save humanity from sin. He GAVE His life on the cross but He IS the risen Lord and King! Again, Lord is who He IS; Savior represents only what He DID for us on the cross. We should know Him, not only as our Savior, but more fully as our present reigning Lord and King. It just so happened that most of the Jews at the time of Christ were far too "religious" by their own way of thinking to even recognize the King—who had been prophesied in the *Scriptures*—when He appeared. That is what such a misguided religious view, based on not seeing "the forest for the trees," does. It the Bible is about a **King**, His **Kingdom**, and His **Royal offspring** puts blinders on people so that they fail to recognize the true Kingdom of God even when it is right before them. Again, it is just a matter of "missing the forest for the trees."

One reference for Jesus coming as King can be found in *Daniel 2:31-45*. Daniel interprets King Nebuchadnezzar's dream about the image representing kingdoms of the earth. In *verse 44*, Daniel says, *"And in the days of these kings the God of Heaven will set up a kingdom which will never be destroyed."* Then he refers to *"the stone cut out of the mountain without hands,"* which is a reference to Jesus the King being born of a virgin. Daniel foretells that the Kingdom that God will set up will be an everlasting Kingdom that will take over the entire earth.

Another prophecy that gives insight into Jesus' purpose for coming can be found in the Book of Isaiah. This particular prophecy tells a great deal about the assignment of the Messiah. *Isaiah 9:6-7* reads,

> *"For a child will be born to us, a son will be given to us; And the government will rest on His shoulders; And His name will be called Wonderful Counselor, Mighty God, Eternal Father, Prince of Peace. There will be no end to the increase of His government or of peace, On the throne of David and over his kingdom, To establish it and to uphold it with justice and righteousness From then on and forevermore. The zeal of the Lord of hosts will accomplish this."*

Notice in this passage of scripture that a *"child is born"* but a *"son is given."* The phrase *"child is born,"* refers to the humanity of Jesus who was birthed by his earthly mother. The *"son is given"* refers to the deity of Jesus, meaning He has always existed with the Father in Heaven. *John 1:1* says, *"In the beginning was the Word, and the Word was with God, and the Word was God.*" Jesus—perfect in all of His ways—always was and always will be! By entering the physical realm in human form—He was able, as "the last Adam, free of sin," to fulfill the legal requirements for accomplishing His purpose of providing propitiation for our sins to redeem and restore us to His Kingdom. Remember, we said that Jesus had to come as a man to get back what the first Adam surrendered, and that is exactly what He did!

Another important phrase can be found in *Isaiah 9:6*: "*... the government will rest on His shoulders.*" Once again, it does not state that the "greatest new religion" will rest on His shoulders. No. It says "government." *Isaiah, chapter 9* is all about a King, His Kingdom and His royal offspring. The word, "government," here, is referring to the Kingdom. And the word "shoulders" is a type and shadow of the children of God, who are the citizens of the Kingdom, and who are also known as the "body of Christ." Shoulders are part of the body and we, as born-again believers who have been given the keys of the Kingdom, are the "body of Christ" (see *1 Corinthians 12:27*). So, Isaiah 9 is effectively saying that "the Kingdom government of God will rest on the shoulders of the body of Christ." We know that the body of Christ is the church! As believers, we are not intended to just be waiting around to go to His Kingdom when our life on earth comes to a close. No. We are already a part of His Kingdom and we have been assigned important work to do!

As all of us who profess the faith go about our daily lives, let this permeate our thoughts: "God's Kingdom is intrinsically dependent upon you and me." As the body of Christ, God's Kingdom—in and on the earth—indeed does rest on our shoulders. We play an important role, being led by the Spirit to do our parts everywhere we go to lift and advance His Kingdom. Wow!

Again, in *Isaiah 9:7*, the prophet proclaims, "*... there will be* *no end to the increase of His government or of peace, on the throne of David and over his kingdom.*" Therefore, this scripture foretells that the government of God would have no end and that Jesus, the King, would come through the bloodline of King David—traceable all the way back to Abraham. As earlier stated, God created a covenant people to establish a royal ancestry for the coming Messiah. With prophecies like these, it is a wonder how so much of the church world—with their vision clouded by their fixed focus on "trees"—has missed seeing the "forest" of the *Bible*. In its full context, the *Bible* is clearly not about religion, as some would think of it. Rather, it is actually about the Kingdom government of God and His Kingdom plans for His creation. Here are several *Old Testament* examples of God described as King:

> *Isaiah 6:5 "Then I said, 'Woe is me, for I am ruined! Because I am a man of unclean lips, And I live among a people of unclean lips; For my eyes have seen the King, the Lord of hosts.'"*

> *Psalms 24:8 "Who is the King of glory? The Lord strong and mighty, The Lord mighty in battle."*

> *Psalms 47:7-8 "For God is the King of all the earth; Sing praises with a skillful psalm. God reigns over the nations, God sits on His holy throne."*

> *Psalms 93:1-2 "The Lord reigns, He is clothed with majesty; The Lord has clothed and girded Himself with strength; Indeed, the world is firmly established, it will not be moved. Your throne is established from of old; You are from everlasting."*

Psalms 95:3 "For the Lord is a great God And a great King above all gods."

Psalms 104:1 "Bless the Lord, O my soul! O Lord my God, You are very great; You are clothed with splendor and majesty."

Psalms 145:1 "I will extol You, my God, O King, And I will bless Your name forever and ever."

Psalms 145:12-13 "To make known to the sons of men Your mighty acts And the glory of the majesty of Your kingdom. Your kingdom is an everlasting kingdom, And Your dominion endures throughout all generations."

Jeremiah 46:18 "As I live," declares the King Whose name is the Lord of hosts..."

Daniel 7:14 "And to Him was given dominion, Glory and a kingdom, That all the peoples, nations and men of every language Might serve Him. His dominion is an everlasting dominion Which will not pass away; And His kingdom is one Which will not be destroyed."

THE ASSIGNMENT OF JESUS

In the first chapter of the *Gospel* of *Matthew*, we find the genealogy of Jesus. This account traces Jesus' bloodline all the way from Abraham through King David and forward to His earthly father, Joseph. (Note: Through her betrothal and eventual marriage to Joseph, Jesus' mother, Mary, along with Jesus, became legally part of the "House of David"). Remember that David was king of the Jews, so Jesus is part of that royal ancestry. Matthew goes on to tell the account of Jesus being conceived by the Holy Spirit and being born of the Virgin Mary. Matthew explains how, after being told in a dream that the child was from God, Joseph stayed with Mary, his wife. And Jesus was called "Immanuel"—which means "God with us."

In *Luke 1:32-33*, the angel said to Mary about the child, "He will be great and will be called the Son of the Most High; and the Lord God will give Him the throne of His father David; and He will reign over the house of Jacob forever, and His kingdom will have no end." So, right here, the angel of the Lord clearly tells Mary that her son, Jesus, will have the throne and His Kingdom will have no end. According to this verse, His Kingdom manifested itself at the time of His birth. Jesus is King; there is no doubt about it.

So, now we have Jesus, as God, wrapped in the flesh of humanity, born into the world system as man, the "Son of man." We know that the shepherds came the night Jesus was born in the manger. Later, as a young toddler about two years old, Jesus was visited by the Magi from the east who came to worship Him, as described in *Matthew 2:1-4*:

> "Now after Jesus was born in Bethlehem of Judea in the days of Herod, the king, magi from the east arrived in Jerusalem, saying, 'Where is He who has been born King of the Jews? For we saw His star in the east and have come to worship Him.' When Herod the king heard this, he was troubled, and all Jerusalem with him. Gathering together all the chief priests and scribes of the people, he inquired of them where the Messiah was to be born."

The Magi belonged to a group of wise men who, for hundreds of years, had been mindful of the prophecies foretelling the birth of the "Messiah King of the Jews" who would be "above all kings." Upon finding Jesus and bowing before Him, the Magi presented Him with treasures consisting of gold, frankincense, and myrrh. Based on the **proper** action when coming into the **presence** of a **king** is to **bow down** the customs of those times, it has been estimated that the value of these gifts would have been no small sum, what today would amount to perhaps several million dollars. Whether you agree with that appraisal or not, one must ask the question, "Why were Herod and all of Jerusalem troubled, if these wise men came to town carrying small gifts commonly depicted in nativity scenes?" These Magi were searching for a special King, one—supreme in authority—who would set up an everlasting Kingdom on the earth. Their gifts would certainly not have been paltry. They would have been appropriately impressive "royal treasures" befitting the "King of kings" whom they had travelled far and wide to honor. What is significant is how they presented their gifts; they bowed and fell to the ground, which would have been the proper practice while in the presence of a king, and they were there to worship and pay tribute to the "King of kings." *Matthew 2:11* says, "*After coming into the house they saw the Child with Mary His mother; and they fell to the ground and worshiped Him. Then, opening their treasures, they presented to Him gifts of gold, frankincense, and myrrh.*" Jesus was in fact the "prophesied King" and these wisest of men recognized and honored Him accordingly.

King Herod was so troubled, in fact, that—under the influence of Satan—he instructed the visiting Magi that they should, after finding the child, report back to him. He lied to them, falsely claiming that he shared their interest in going to worship the child. His actual intention was to slay the Christ Child; however, the Magi were forewarned by an angel not to return to Herod.

After the Magi had departed to return to their home country, an angel of the Lord appeared to Joseph in a dream, saying, "*Get up! Take the child and His mother and flee to Egypt, and remain there until I tell you; for Herod is going to search for the child to destroy Him*" (*Matthew 2:17*). So, Mary and Joseph—well endowed for making a long journey and for getting all set for life in another country, having had received treasures from the Magi—did as the angel instructed them. They took their young child, Jesus, to live for a while in Egypt. The *Bible* tells us that Herod was so enraged by the Magi's failure to report back to him that he ordered every male child born in Bethlehem, two years of age and under, to be put to death. Just another attempt by the enemy to thwart the plans of God.

PREACH THE KINGDOM

Nearly three decades after the visit of the Magi, a man called John the Baptist could be heard preaching to crowds who gathered to hear him in the wilderness. This righteous man, who was Jesus' cousin, went about proclaiming, *"Repent, for the kingdom of heaven is at hand" (Matthew 3:2)*. The *Bible* tells us that John was the one who came, before Jesus, to "make straight the way of the Lord" (Mark 1:3). In essence, he was preparing people to receive the message of the coming Messiah. The word "repent" used here literally means "change your thinking."

Unfortunately, the word "repent" has been hollowed out into a religious term associated with the connotation of guilt, specifically the emotion of sadness resulting from feeling sorry about having sinned. The full meaning of repent is much more empowering than that! When considering the "forest" of the *Bible*, we observe that John the Baptist is actually proclaiming, "It's time to change how you think about things, because the Kingdom is here now!" He was imploring the people to arrest their ungodly thoughts and to think as God thinks—Kingdom thoughts! Real repentance involves a renewing of the mind to what I like to call "God's Kingdom thinking."

Matthew 3:13-17 gives an account of John the Baptist baptizing Jesus with water. As Jesus emerged from the river, "*... heaven opened and He saw the Spirit of God descending as a dove and alighting on Him, and behold, a voice from Heaven said, 'This is My beloved Son, in whom I am well-pleased.'*" So, we see that, upon His baptism, Jesus receives the Spirit of God and now will be led by the Spirit. *"Then Jesus was led by the Spirit into the wilderness to be tempted by the devil." (Matthew 4:1 NIV)*.

For the full account of the temptation of Jesus, read Chapter 4 of the *Gospel of Matthew*, but, for now, let us focus primarily on *Matthew 4:8-9: "Again, the devil took Him to a very high mountain and showed Him all the kingdoms of the world and their glory; and he said to Him, 'All these things I will give You, if you fall down and worship me.'*" So, even with the temptation of our Lord by the enemy, we see the "forest" of the Kingdom. The devil is saying, "Jesus worship me, and I'll give you all these kingdoms in the world!" Let us recall that, since Adam had handed his dominion over the world's system to the enemy, Satan held the legal right to offer the world's kingdoms to Jesus (see *Luke 4:5-6*). This has been misinterpreted as the devil "lying" in an attempt to try to tempt Jesus; however, that simply lacks validity. If

God is all about re-establishing His kingdom on earth! That's why Jesus preached the kingdom.

the devil had been making pretences about his ability to give Jesus the kingdoms of the world, then Jesus would have undoubtedly recognized that Satan would be unable to deliver upon his offer, so there would have been no actual temptation involved. The *Bible* would not say that Jesus "was tempted" if were untrue. No. The devil was not faking, and this was designed to truly place Jesus under great temptation. We see from this account that the devil maintained his prideful place and was continually consumed with the idea of God worshiping him. Satan passionately desired that the King should bow down to him. Remember why he was cast out from heaven in the first place. He wanted to exalt his throne above the Most High. It stands to reason that the enemy presumed that, since he had caused the first Adam to fall, he could probably get this "last Adam" to do so as well.

Again, it is important to notice that Satan did not tempt Jesus by offering to put him at the pinnacle of the "religious world." That would not have been a real temptation for Jesus, because He did not come for the purpose of either starting or becoming the subject of a religion. He was destined to be the King of kings whose government would have no end! Praise God! Jesus knew this, and He evoked the Word, the *Holy Scriptures*, to deflect Satan's temptations. (See *Luke 4: 4, 8, and 12*). This illustrates how we obtain victory in the Kingdom, by knowing and being able to apply the powerful *Words* of the King!

In the study and application of the *Scriptures*, it pretty much goes without saying that, for something to be properly weighed as sound doctrine, there must be actual, ample scripture to adequately support it. In *2 Corinthians 13:1*, Paul tells us, *"Every fact is to be confirmed by the testimony of two or three witnesses."'* Anytime I preach or teach from the *Word of God*, I use at least two or three "witnesses" (supporting *Scriptures*). There is nothing like being thorough when discussing something as precious and profound as the *Word of God*. I strive to be diligent when attempting to show the whole "forest" of the *Bible*, keeping the Word in proper context. Therefore, let us examine multiple teachings spoken by Jesus, Himself.

After His temptation in the wilderness, Jesus returned to Galilee and began preaching, saying, *"The time is fulfilled, and the Kingdom of God is at hand; repent and believe in the Gospel" (Mark 1:14-15)*. So, from the very beginning of His public ministry, Jesus was teaching and proclaiming the Kingdom of God. He was declaring the same message that John the Baptist proclaimed, by telling people to "change their thinking" for the "Kingdom is here!"

One very significant way the Kingdom changes people's thinking is in the area of anxiety. *Matthew Chapter 6* gives the account of Jesus teaching regarding worry and anxiety in life. In *Matthew 6:25-34*, Jesus says,

> *"For this reason I say to you, do not be worried about your life, as to what you will eat or what you will drink; nor for your body, as to what you will put on. Is not life more than food, and the body more than clothing? Look at the birds of the air, that they do not sow, nor reap nor gather into barns, and yet your heavenly Father feeds them. Are you not worth much more than they? And who of you by being worried can add a single hour to his life? And why are you worried about clothing? Observe how the lilies of the field grow; they do not toil nor do they spin, yet I say to you that not even Solomon in all his glory clothed himself like one of these. But if God so clothes the grass of the field, which is alive today and tomorrow is thrown into the furnace, will He not much more clothe you? You of little faith! Do not worry then, saying, 'What will we eat?' or 'What will we drink?' or*

'What will we wear for clothing?' For the Gentiles eagerly seek all these things; for your heavenly Father knows that you need all these things. But seek first His kingdom and His righteousness, and all these things will be added to you. So do not worry about tomorrow; for tomorrow will care for itself. Each day has enough trouble of its own."

Jesus instructs us that all the basic things that the world is concerned about, such as food and clothing, are no longer to be of any concern to citizens of His Kingdom. He is not denying the importance of those things; however, He says the Father already knows that we need them, and He will provide what we need if we "seek first the Kingdom of God and His righteousness." Just as God provides for the birds of the air, He will always supply our needs, if we remain in good standing with His government. As Kingdom citizens, our focus should be on the advancement of the Kingdom and on keeping our right standing with our King. That is why we take one day at a time, serving God wholeheartedly without becoming anxious. Only when we are truly seeking His Kingdom will we have no reason to worry or to become anxious, as we trust the King to add all necessities to us. The Kingdom thought process of fully trusting and putting all faith in the King is entirely different from most of the world, as well as also being different from the practices of a significant number of believers today who fail to "see the forest." To enjoy the benefits of living the Kingdom lifestyle, it is important that we renew our thinking daily, truly focusing on the Kingdom of God and His righteousness as that which must remain foremost in our lives. *Romans 12:2 (NIV)* says,

"Do not conform to the pattern of this world, but be transformed by the renewing of your mind. Then you will be able to test and approve what God's will is—his good, pleasing and perfect will."

Jesus talked about the Kingdom of God all the time. This message consumed Him. There are over 130 references to the Kingdom in the Four *Gospel*s alone. In fact, from my own studies, I have noticed that, nearly every time Jesus spoke in public, *His Word*s were related in some way to His Kingdom. The only times that He spoke publicly about something unrelated to His Kingdom were situations where He was asked specific questions concerning other topics. Many times the motives behind such questioning were insincere, aimed only with the intent of trying to trick and trap Him, and these were not topics about which he necessarily desired to speak. His favorite topic to expound upon was the Kingdom of God, and He taught so frequently about things related to the Kingdom that His disciples were also preoccupied with everything He had to say on the subject. In effect, by talking about the Kingdom, He was helping the disciples to "change their thinking." Here are some of the many examples of Jesus' Kingdom ministry:

Matthew 4:17, "From that time Jesus began to preach and say, 'Repent, for the kingdom of heaven is at hand.'"

Matthew 10:7, "And as you go, preach, saying, 'The kingdom of heaven is at hand.'"

Matthew 12:28, "But if I cast out demons by the Spirit of God, then the Kingdom of God has come upon you."

Matthew 18:23, "For this reason the kingdom of heaven may be compared to a king who wished to settle accounts with his slaves."

Matthew 24:14, "This Gospel of the kingdom shall be preached in the whole world as a testimony to all the nations, and then the end will come."

Luke 4:43, "But He said to them, 'I must preach the Kingdom of God to the other cities also, for I was sent for this purpose.'"

Luke 8:1, "Soon afterwards, He began going around from one city and village to another, proclaiming and preaching the Kingdom of God. The twelve were with Him."

Luke 9:11, "But the crowds were aware of this and followed Him; and welcoming them, He began speaking to them about the Kingdom of God and curing those who had need of healing."

Luke 12:31-32, "But seek His kingdom, and these things will be added to you. Do not be afraid, little flock, for your Father has chosen gladly to give you the kingdom."

Luke 18:17, "Truly I say to you, whoever does not receive the Kingdom of God like a child will not enter it at all."

Luke 22:29, " ... and just as My Father has granted Me a kingdom, I grant you."

These represent just a few examples of the numerous scriptures that demonstrate Jesus' primary purpose and intent. As we said, nearly every time Jesus publicly preached it was about the

Kingdom of God. It was His mission to bring the Kingdom back to humanity and to reunite humanity with their Creator in Heaven. That is the true *Gospel* message: "The Kingdom of Heaven is at Hand!"

Many Christians today have their eyes fixed on going to Heaven when they die, which is certainly great to ponder over. However, when looking through the context of the Kingdom at the "forest," we see that God is far more consumed with using us to bring Heaven to earth than He is with our desire to escape to Heaven. In fact, it is here on the planet that Jesus Christ will set up His rule and reign for one thousand years. In a later chapter, we will talk about the events that will happen after the millennial reign of Christ—what will ultimately transpire regarding Heaven and the earth.

God is all about re-establishing His Kingdom in and on the earth, and that is why Jesus was constantly preaching the "Kingdom message." Even after Jesus was resurrected, He taught about the Kingdom. *Acts 1:3* says,

> *"To these He also presented Himself alive after His suffering, by many convincing proofs, appearing to them over a period of forty days and speaking of the things concerning the Kingdom of God."*

He desired for the "Kingdom message" to be at the forefront of His disciples' minds. His commission to "go" was with the intent for them to preach the Kingdom, and preach the Kingdom they did! *Acts 8:12 (NASB)* records Philip's message to Samaria:

> *"But when they believed Philip preaching the good news about the Kingdom of God and the name of Jesus Christ, they were being baptized, men and women alike."*

MIRACLES AND SIGNS

Jesus' miracles, signs, and wonders are among the more emphasized aspects of His life recorded from His time on earth. From the instant that the Holy Spirit descended upon Him, it became clear that Jesus operated with the authority and power of God. This divine authority was why He was able to perform wonderous acts. To grasp the significance of this in the full context of the *Bible*, it is necessary to recall, in *Genesis 1:26*, what God gave to Adam. *"Then God said, 'Let Us make man in Our image, according to Our likeness; and let them rule over the fish of the sea and over the birds of the sky and over the cattle and over all the earth, and over every creeping thing that creeps on the earth.'"* Remember. Adam sinned by disobeying God, thereby, giving up the position of dominion bestowed upon him by his Creator. But Jesus, Whom the *Scriptures* refer to as *"the last Adam,"* had authority to operate in the dominion that the "first Adam" had given up. This was why Jesus was able to perform miraculous signs and wonders.

Beginning with the very first miracle that Jesus performed, we see many examples of His dominion over creation. In *John 2, 6-10,* Jesus exercised His dominion power by transforming water into wine at the marriage feast of Cana, demonstrating His authority over water. He accessed dominion authority from the unseen realm, and the physical realm obeyed His commands. *Matthew 21:19* describes an example of Jesus exercising dominion over living things: *"Seeing a lone fig tree by the road, He came to it and found nothing on it except leaves only; and He said to it, 'No longer shall there ever be any fruit from you.'"* Within the short span of 24 hours, the fig tree withered. Jesus gave orders to a tree, and it died. Let us examine this. He did not cut the tree down, nor did He poison the root system. No. He merely spoke, and it happened. Now, that is dominion power! Trees grow on the earth; therefore, the tree reacted because Jesus had authority and power over it.

Another example of Jesus operating from the position of dominion which Adam gave up can be found in *Luke 5:1-11.* In this passage, Jesus uses Simon Peter's fishing boat in which to stand, in order to avoid the crush of people while preaching to the crowds. Afterwards, He tells Simon Peter to go out and let down his nets for a catch. Simon Peter replies, *"Master, we worked hard all night and caught nothing, but I will do as You say and let down the nets."* Luke reports that, when they followed Jesus' instructions, they captured so many fish that their nets began to break. They had to summon some of their friends to bring over another boat to help them, because their vessel was beginning to sink low in the water under the weight of all the fish they had netted. Wow! Jesus exercised dominion authority "over the fish of the sea." Even after these professional fishermen had toiled all night and caught nothing, with a single command Jesus was able to supply for them more fish than their boats could handle.

On a different occasion, Jesus exercised His dominion authority over creation by calming the wind and waves. He and His disciples were traveling by boat across the sea, when Jesus fell asleep. After a while, a sudden wind storm started acting up, and the disciples grew fearful. *Mark 4:37-39* describes what took place: *"And there arose a fierce gale of wind, and the waves were breaking over the boat so much that the boat was already filling up. Jesus Himself was in the stern, asleep on the cushion; and they woke Him and said to Him, 'Teacher, do You not care that we are perishing?' And He got up and rebuked the wind and said to the sea, "Hush, be still." And the wind died down, and it became perfectly calm."* So, again, just by *His Word*s, Jesus asserted dominion authority over the natural elements of the world. It appeared as if the storm realized that He held dominion over it, because it obeyed His command.

There is another account where Jesus fed more than 5,000 people by miraculously multiplying five loaves and two fish. *John 6:11-14* describes this in detail:

> *"Jesus then took the loaves, and having given thanks, He distributed to those who were seated; likewise also of the fish as much as they wanted. When they were filled, He said to His disciples, 'Gather up the leftover fragments so that nothing will be lost.' So they gathered them up and filled twelve baskets with fragments from the five barley loaves*

JESUS OPERATED IN THE DOMINION THAT ADAM HAD LOST

which were left over by those who had eaten. Therefore when the people saw the sign which He had performed, they said, "This is truly the Prophet, who is to come into the world."

This is just another example of Jesus' ability to rule over things of the earth.

There are numerous accounts of Jesus' performing miraculous acts of healing, attesting to His dominion over things of the earth. Since Jesus operated in the authority to exercise dominion over the earth, no wonder He could speak by the direction of the Spirit and people would be healed. After all, was man not formed from the dust of the earth? Paul called the body an "earthly tent" in *2 Corinthians 5:1*: *"For we know that if the earthly tent which is our house is torn down, we have a building from God, a house not made with hands, eternal in the heavens."*

All of these miracles and healings demonstrate the rulership that Jesus, as "King of kings," holds over creation. He exercised (and still exercises) His dominion to restore what the devil had damaged. In fact, in *1 John 3:8*, it says that Jesus came to "destroy" the works of the devil. Below are a few examples of Jesus thwarting the enemy by healing people:

Mark 1:30-31 "Now Simon's mother-in-law was lying sick with a fever; and immediately they spoke to Jesus about her. And He came to her and raised her up, taking her by the hand, and the fever left her, and she waited on them."

Mark 1:40-42 "And a leper came to Jesus, beseeching Him and falling on his knees before Him, and saying, 'If You are willing, You can make me clean.' Moved with compassion,

Jesus stretched out His hand and touched him, and said to him, "I am willing; be cleansed." Immediately the leprosy left him and he was cleansed."

Mathew 9:6-8 "But so that you may know that the Son of Man has authority on earth to forgive sins"—then He said to the paralytic, 'Get up, pick up your bed and go home.' And he got up and went home. But when the crowds saw this, they were awestruck, and glorified God, who had given such authority to men."

John 5:6-9 "When Jesus saw him lying there, and knew that he had already been a long time in that condition, He said to him, 'Do you wish to get well?' The sick man answered Him, "Sir, I have no man to put me into the pool when the water is stirred up, but while I am coming, another steps down before me." Jesus said to him, 'Get up, pick up your pallet and walk.' Immediately the man became well, and picked up his pallet and began to walk."

THE LORD'S PRAYER

Another important aspect of Jesus' ministry can be found in the manner in which He models how to pray to our Father in Heaven, as accounted in the *Gospel of Matthew*. Let us focus on "The Lord's Prayer" through the lens of the Kingdom. In *Matthew 6:9-13*, Jesus taught His disciples,

> "*Pray, then, in this way: 'Our Father who is in heaven, Hallowed be Your name. Your kingdom come. Your will be done, On earth as it is in heaven. Give us this day our daily*

bread. And forgive us our debts, as we also have forgiven our debtors. And do not lead us into temptation, but deliver us from evil. For Yours is the kingdom and the power and the glory forever. Amen.'" One of the first things that Jesus expresses in His exemplary prayer is "Your kingdom come. Your will be done, On earth as it is in heaven."

Jesus is teaching His disciples how to pray to our Heavenly Father, and He shows them how to pray for "the Kingdom." Notice the phrase " *...on earth as it is in heaven.*" This indicates God's desire to influence the earth through the Kingdom culture of Heaven.

As mentioned earlier, many Christians today seem to focus much of their mindset regarding their faith on one day escaping earth in order to reach God's Kingdom in Heaven. Well, it would be a good idea to take careful notice that, in the "Lord's Prayer," (*Matthew 6:9-13*), Jesus shows us that God is more interested in using us to bring Heaven to earth than he is in our interest in going to heaven! He desires for his Kingdom to be made manifest in its fullness here—in and on the earth. We must not ignore that He expects us to be active every day of our lives as citizens of his Kingdom, fulfilling his purpose for our lives! Our daily mindset and priorities need to match up with what Jesus is telling us to pray for: that "His Kingdom come," here, in and on the earth. Now rather than later!

Even at the conclusion of the prayer which he taught his disciples to pray, Jesus again mentions the Kingdom, when He says, *"For Yours is the kingdom, and the glory, and the power forever."* In fact, the Kingdom is the only thing that Jesus mentions twice in His exemplary prayer. Just another indicator that both Jesus and the Father are "Kingdom-minded." God knows that—when His Kingdom is evident in the world, as it is made manifest through the lifestyle of its

Your **kingdom come** Your **will** be **done** on **earth** as it is in **heaven** citizens—people will be drawn to Him because of His immeasurable goodness. Contrary to the teachings which focus on "trees" while missing the "forest," Jesus did not come just to save us from hell but also to restore the Kingdom of God in and on the earth. That is why Jesus taught us to pray to our Father in Heaven that His " ... Kingdom come ... " Hallelujah!

JESUS BEFORE PILATE

No passage of scripture better illustrates Jesus' Kingship than *John 18:33-37*. It tells how, after being arrested, Jesus is brought by the high priests before Pontius Pilate who, after questioning Him, determines that Jesus is a king. Being a Roman governor, Pilate certainly is well familiar with governments and how they operate, but Jesus explains to him that His Kingdom is different, that it is of another realm. This is how John describes the exchange:

"Therefore Pilate entered again into the Praetorium, and summoned Jesus and said to Him, 'Are You the King of the Jews?' Jesus answered, "Are you saying this on your own initiative, or did others tell you about Me?" Pilate answered, 'I am not a Jew, am I? Your own nation and the chief priests delivered You to me; what have You done?' Jesus answered, "My kingdom is not of this world. If My kingdom were of this world, then My servants would be fighting so that I would not be handed over to the Jews; but as it is, My kingdom is not of this realm." Therefore Pilate said to Him, 'So You are a king?' Jesus answered, " You say correctly that I am a king. For this I have been born, and for this I have come into the world, to testify to the truth. Everyone who is of the truth hears My voice."

John records how Pilate asks Jesus directly, *"Are You the King of the Jews?"* Notice that the Roman governor does not ask Jesus if He is attempting to appeal to crowds of followers in order to establish himself an up-and-coming, influential religious leader. That is of no concern to him. As a high government official with allegiance to Rome, Pilate is chiefly concerned about whether or not this man brought before him has any designs on becoming a king. He has no interest in whether or not Jesus may be starting some new religion or religious sect. If Jesus has just come to start a new religion, then the sign Pilate later would have placed above Jesus's head on the cross would have read: "Jesus the Nazarene: Great Religious Leader of the Jews." No. When ordering the sign to be made, Pilot intends to mock Jesus' true purpose by having it written: *"Jesus the Nazarene: King of the Jews"* (*John 19:19*). This also serves as a warning to any others who would attempt, in any way, to challenge the throne of Caesar. The sign that Pilate has crafted is designed to mock the very substance of everything that Jesus has preached—"His Kingdom."

I really love how Jesus responds when the highest Roman official in the land questions Him about His Kingship. He asks Pontius Pilate, *"Are you saying this on your own initiative or did others tell you about Me?"* In other words, "Did you come to this conclusion on your own accord or did someone tell you?" Man...I mean...talk about being calm under pressure. Jesus is fully aware that Pilate, as governor of all Judaea, will be making the final pronouncement to reveal His fate. While standing before this powerful ruler, Jesus remains fearless and undaunted, demonstrating the confidence and stature befitting a king. Jesus knows that He has an assignment with a purpose to be carried out, and He does not flinch!

Pilate answers Jesus, saying, *"I am not a Jew, am, I? Your own nation and chief priests delivered You to me; what have You done?"* (*John 18:35*). Then Jesus tells him directly, leaving no doubt about Who He is or why He has come. In *verse 36* Jesus proclaims, *"My kingdom is not of this world. If My kingdom were of this world, then My servants would be fighting so that I would not be handed over to the Jews; but as it is My kingdom is not of this realm."*

Jesus is pointing out to Pilate that His Kingdom is of a spiritual realm—not "of the world." However, while it is not "of the world," His spiritual Kingdom is "in the world." By saying that His Kingdom is not "of the world," Jesus is explaining that His Kingdom operates in a different realm than the "kingdoms of this world." In other words, the realm of the Kingdom of God exists and operates differently than the realm of worldly kingdoms; otherwise, his enemies never could have captured and detained Jesus in the first place. We know from *Matthew 26:53* that, if He had so chosen, Jesus could have summoned a dozen legions of angels to show up and rescue Him. Just consider for a moment what it would have meant for twelve legions of angels

PILATE DID NOT ASK JESUS IF HE WAS THE NEXT RELIGIOUS LEADER OR IF HE WAS ATTEMPTING TO RALLY A RELIGIOUS FOLLOWING OF PEOPLE to have actually come to earth to fight. It could have easily resulted in the annihilation of the entire Roman Empire. One angel, according to *Isaiah 37:36*, slew 185,000 men in one night. Standing before Pilate, Jesus certainly has at his disposal an army that could easily defend Him; however, as He states, His Kingdom operates differently than all of those on the earth. In an earthly kingdom, it is unlikely that a powerful king would choose to sacrifice himself for the good of the people. This just shows us what an awesome King we serve!

After Jesus' remarks regarding the nature of His Kingdom, Pilate then asks Him point-blankly, *"You are a king?"* To which Jesus answers directly, *"You say correctly I am a king."* There you have it, the end of any debate. Jesus calls Himself King, despite the fact that saying so will cost Him His life. He replies, *"For this I have been born, and for this I have come into the world, to testify to the truth. Everyone who is of the truth hears My voice."* Jesus tells us here that He came into the world to testify of the truth. What truth? The truth of the Kingdom of God!

God is a good Father who loves His creation, including all of humanity, and He desires that all would repent and enter into His Kingdom. Jesus was sent to destroy the works of the devil by bringing the Kingdom of God back to earth! The entire account of Jesus' exchange with Pontius Pilate is just more proof of this fact. There is no denying it. Jesus is King! He came so we can be part of His Kingdom! Amen!!

FILLED THE WHOLE EARTH

It amazes me how many persons appear to be just waiting or hoping to get to Heaven. When we look back at Adam in the Garden of Eden—before he rebelled against God by partaking of the forbidden fruit—it is evident that Adam was not longing to leave the earth to go to Heaven. In fact, *Genesis 3:8* clearly shows that Heaven came to earth: *"They heard the sound of the Lord God walking in the garden in the cool of the day..."*

By pointing out that Adam had no interest in going to Heaven, I do not wish to infer that going to heaven is in any manner unimportant. I wholeheartedly believe that—when people pass away, transitioning from this life on earth—they do go to Heaven. Of course, I am only speaking of those who have repented, confessed Jesus as their Lord, and have lived as faithful and fruitful born-again citizens of His Kingdom. I stand in agreement with the Apostle Paul, when he says, in *2 Corinthians 5:8*, "*We are of good courage, I say, and prefer rather to be absent from the body and to be at home with the Lord.*" However, we know that, right up to the end of his life, Paul tirelessly devoted himself to his ministry of spreading the *Good News of the Kingdom* far and wide here on the earth. There are many Christians who appear to be content with the idea of biding their time, with minimal interest in God's Kingdom here, in and on the earth, while waiting to desert the planet for Heaven. Perhaps it would behove them to consider whether or not God shares in their idea of being so focused on abandoning the earth that He created for them. Let us not forget that Jesus taught that we should pray to the Father that "*Your Kingdom come*" (*Matthew 6:9-10*). We all need to recognize from our study of the *Scriptures* that God's plans for rebuilding His Kingdom, in and on the earth, remain unfinished, and that we are called to help fulfill His plans in our daily lives. And this is not a part-time assignment. God desires for His Kingdom to be made manifest throughout the earth. We are compelled to make it our highest priority to help accomplish this purpose! We are not called to bide our time here on earth dreaming about a life to come. God has plans for us to be Kingdom spreaders, here and now!

In the prophecy given to Daniel, we can see an amazing truth in light of the Kingdom. Look at *Daniel 2:31-35*:

> "*You, O king, were looking and behold, there was a single great statue; that statue, which was large and of extraordinary splendor, was standing in front of you, and its appearance*

was awesome. The head of that statue was made of fine gold, its breast and its arms of silver, its belly and its thighs of bronze, its legs of iron, its feet partly of iron and partly of clay. You continued looking until a stone was cut out without hands, and it struck the statue on its feet of iron and clay and crushed them. Then the iron, the clay, the bronze, the silver and the gold were crushed all at the same time and became like chaff from the summer threshing floors; and the wind carried them away so that not a trace of them was found. But the stone that struck the statue became a great mountain and filled the whole earth."

Bible scholars agree that the phrase "... *a stone was cut out without hands* ..." is a direct reference to Jesus. He is the One born of a virgin and known as the *"chief cornerstone."* In verse 35, notice what happens with the "stone." It does not leave the earth once it destroys all the other kingdoms; rather, it fills "the whole earth." God is not abandoning His creation!

As we stated earlier, most of the preaching and teaching in the church today appears to come from only part of the *Bible*—from *Genesis 3*, "after the fall of man," through *Revelation 20*, "the book of life and the lake of fire"—while, at best, barely touching on the first two chapters and the last two chapters of *God's Word*. This limited focus prevents a full view of "the forest." We have already discussed the profound importance of the first two chapters of the *Bible*, which lay the context for all of *God's Word*. But what about the last two chapters? These two chapters talk about what occurs after the following events: the "catching away" of the church, the "judgment seat of Christ," the "Tribulation Period," the "binding of Satan during the millennial reign of Christ," the "release of Satan for Armageddon," the "judgment at the great white throne" and the "second death which is the lake of fire." Then, the last two chapters of the *Bible* outline God's ultimate plans for His Kingdom of which we need to be aware, because it is important for us to try to grasp all of God's plans for His Kingdom revealed to us in the *Scriptures* by Him, leaving out nothing. Otherwise, we will be unable to clearly see "the forest."

Let us look at *Revelation 21:1-2*:

> *"Then I saw a new heaven and a new earth; for the first heaven and the first earth passed away, and there is no longer any sea. And I saw the holy city, new Jerusalem, coming down out of heaven from God, made ready as a bride adorned for her husband."*

Do you see what this says?! Then, ask yourself the question: "If we are going to be living forever with the Lord far away in Heaven, why is this telling of a new earth?"

The *Word of God* clearly shows Jesus came not just to save and restore us, but His purpose included saving and restoring the planet as well. Look at *Romans 8:18-22 (NLT)*:

> *"Yet what we suffer now is nothing compared to the glory he will reveal to us later. For all creation is waiting eagerly for that future day when God will reveal who his children really are. Against its will, all creation was subjected to God's curse. But with eager hope, the creation looks forward to the day when it will join God's children in glorious freedom from death and decay. For we know that all creation has been groaning as in the pains of childbirth right up to the present time."*

God always planned to restore all of His creation back to His original design and purpose.

if we are only living in Heaven forever with the Lord why is there a new earth?

The Apostle Peter clearly embraced the revelation of the "new earth." In *2 Peter 3:10-13*, he writes:

> *"But the day of the Lord will come like a thief, in which the heavens will pass away with a roar and the elements will be destroyed with intense heat, and the earth and its works will be burned up. Since all these things are to be destroyed in this way, what sort of people ought you to be in holy conduct and godliness, looking for and hastening the coming of the day of God, because of which the heavens will be destroyed by burning, and the elements will melt with intense heat! But according to His promise we are looking for new heavens and a new earth [emphasis added], in which righteousness dwells."*

Now, please allow me to redirect your attention to *Revelation 21:2*. Notice how the "new Jerusalem" will be "coming down out of heaven." The place that God has prepared for us is actually coming to the "new earth." At that time, the whole earth will be filled with His glory! Hallelujah! As you then progress further into the chapter, focusing on *verse 24*, you will identify how King Jesus and His royal offspring will enjoy dominion in the "new earth" to come. That will be our purpose in His Kingdom in the "new earth," to reign with Him for all eternity. *Revelation 21:24-26* states,

> *"The nations will walk by its light, and the kings of the earth will bring their glory into it. In the daytime (for there will be no night there) its gates will never be closed; and they will bring the glory and the honor of the nations into it ... "*

At this point, the *Scriptures* ring loud and clear concerning Jesus.

He is the *"King of kings and the Lord of lords."* There will be total restoration of all creation. We, who serve the King, will exist forever on a "new earth," and we will enjoy access to Heaven—just as Adam did before his fall. It will be the King, His Kingdom, and His royal offspring!

We can understand why even those who remain separated from the Lord cling to the hope of a new and better government that will bring about a better world. The empty place in the human heart is the absence of the Kingdom! It is exciting to know from the full context of the *Holy Scriptures* that God has plans to create a "new Heaven" and a "new earth" where we will reign with King Jesus forever!

RIGHT STANDING WITH GOD

As we have already learned from our contextual study of *God's Word*, when the first Adam fell from his place of dominion, humanity lost its right-standing with the King. Later, God established a covenant with a chosen nation; however, the sinful nature of the people repeatedly got in the way. Then, under a new and better covenant, Jesus came as the "last Adam" to restore the Kingdom back to the planet! Blameless, because He lived free from sin, Jesus— through His death, burial, and resurrection—paid the penalty for sin and bridged the gap between God and humanity!

It is through Jesus' merciful and graceful gift of salvation that humankind can be redeemed, made righteous, and afforded access to God. Once we have received Christ as our Lord and Savior, becoming reborn into the Kingdom of God, then we must learn what God expects of us in our daily lives. We are called out of darkness into the light, out of a worldly lifestyle into a new and better life! It will not work to attempt to straddle the fence. You simply cannot enjoy a right relationship with the Lord while trying to keep one leg in the world and one in the Kingdom. In *John 17:16*, Jesus speaks about His followers while praying to His Heavenly Father. He says, "*They are not of the world, just as I am not of the world.*" The Kingdom lifestyle is about being "all in!"

In *Matthew 7:21 (NKJV)*, Jesus warns, "*Not everyone who says to Me, 'Lord, Lord,' shall enter the kingdom of heaven, but he who does the will of My Father in heaven.*" The government of the Kingdom has guidelines and regulations put in place to ensure order, just as with any other government. These guidelines, when honored and adhered to, release the favor of the King toward His citizens. It is important to understand that all citizens of God's Kingdom have a calling and a duty to embrace a Godly lifestyle, as outlined in the *Bible*. The Apostle Paul tells us, in *2 Corinthians 5:17 (NKJV)*, "Therefore, if anyone is in Christ, he is a new creation; old things have passed away; behold, all things have become new." And, again, in *Romans 12:2 (NKJV)*, he writes, "*And do not be conformed to this world, but be transformed by the renewing of your mind, that you may prove what is that good and acceptable and perfect will of God.*" To help us master the Kingdom lifestyle, God gave us the Holy Spirit and the *Scriptures* to teach and help us in the renewing of our minds. Jesus promised, in *John 14:26*, "*But the Helper, the Holy Spirit, whom the Father will send in My name, He will teach you all things, and bring to your remembrance all that I said to you."*

As mentioned earlier, the first laws were given to the nation of Israel through Moses and were designed to ultimately show that the people needed a Savior, since no one could measure up to *The Law* in its entirety. As a result, no one could ever earn God's righteousness. As Romans 3:20 (NLT) declares, "For no one can ever be made right with God by doing what *The Law* commands. *The Law* simply shows us how sinful we are." Humanity had to have a Savior come to pay the penalty for Adam's treason. Jesus was the perfect Lamb, the sinless Sacrifice that the Father sent to purchase humanity back.

In *Matthew 5:17-18*, Jesus said, *"Do not think that I came to abolish The Law or the Prophets; I did not come to abolish but to fulfill. For truly I say to you, until heaven and earth pass away, not the smallest letter or stroke shall pass from The Law until all is accomplished."* We clearly see that *The Law*, itself, is not done away with; rather, it is fulfilled through Jesus Christ. When Jesus was asked which commandment was the greatest, He replied, *"You shall love the Lord your God with all your heart, and with all your soul, and with all your mind. This is the great and foremost commandment. The second is like it, You shall love your neighbor as yourself. On these two commandments depend the whole Law and the Prophets"* (*Matthew 22:37-40*).

As Jesus traveled and taught, He explained that keeping *The Law* was not just about doing the outward actions; it was about the inward intentions of man. In other words, God looks at the heart of each person; He examines our motives, not just our actions. It is possible to obey *The Law* superficially, while one's heart is still far from God. *Matthew 15:8 (NIV)* says, *"These people honor Me with their lips, but their hearts are far from Me."* God has absolutely no interest in good behavior with impure motives. No. He wants our hearts to be pure and righteous before Him. That is when we are truly in right-

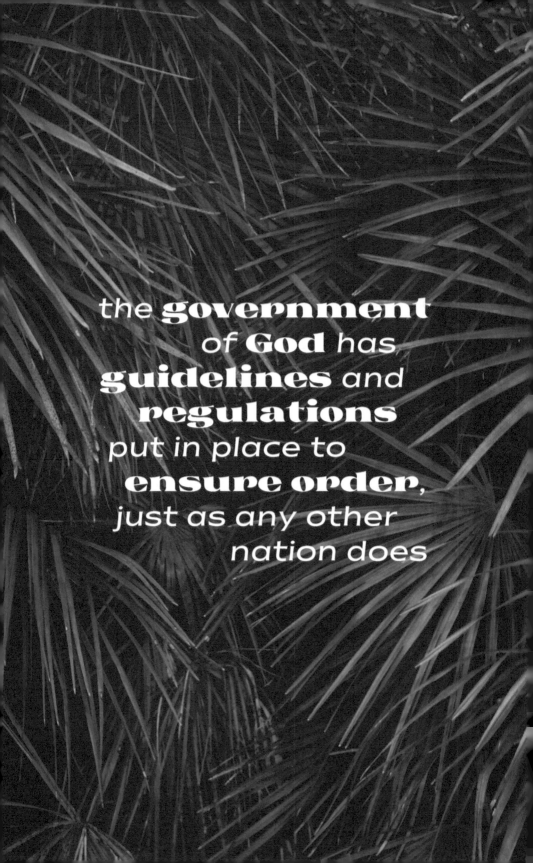

the **government** of **God** has **guidelines** and **regulations** put in place to **ensure order,** just as any other nation does standing with His governing authority. We must keep our hearts soft and contrite, as we seek to do His will.

No other government on earth can discern the true intentions of a person's heart. Think about it. Drivers can obey the speed limit, while feeling disgruntled—even cursing the county government for making them have to drive so slowly. Citizens can obediently pay taxes to the Internal Revenue Service (IRS), while complaining about being over-taxed. These types of behaviors happen all the time in natural governments, but that kind of attitude proves unacceptable in God's Kingdom.

God is King and, as our King, He desires for us to want to serve, obey, and emulate Him, keeping our hearts cheerful and contrite. That is why He gave humankind "free will." He is looking for a citizenship who desires His blessings and loves Him for Who and What He is, not because they are forced to obey Him. That is what separates *The Laws* of the Kingdom from those of the world. In God's Kingdom, it is all about the intentions of the heart. The reason so many of the religious leaders of Jesus' time hated Jesus was because He identified their impure heart motives. In *Matthew 5:27-28*, Jesus says,

> *"You have heard that it was said, 'You shall not commit adultery'; but I say to you that everyone who looks at a woman with lust for her has already committed adultery with her in his heart."*

Jesus is basically saying, "You may not have physically committed adultery but, even so, your lustful appraisal of another woman amounts to the same thing!" He is identifying the necessity of striving to keep our hearts pure and contrite.

In *2 Corinthians 10:3-5 (BBE)*, the Apostle Paul states,

"For though we may be living in the flesh, we are not fighting after the way of the flesh For the arms with which we are fighting are not those of the flesh, but are strong before God for the destruction of high places; Putting an end to reasonings, and every high thing which is lifted up against the knowledge of God, and causing every thought to come under the authority of Christ; ... "

In essence—now that the Kingdom of God is here—we must not only demonstrate righteous actions; just as importantly, we must strive to constantly keep our hearts and thoughts right before God. If our hearts and thoughts are in the wrong place, our actions will not win favor with the King. Therefore, to operate successfully in the Kingdom of God, each of us must work to renew our minds with the full *Word of God*, embracing righteousness in how we conduct our lives—most importantly, always seeking to keep a contrite and pure heart before our King. The heart of a Kingdom citizen hungers after righteousness. Obedience to the King is how we show our love of God and how we maintain right-standing with His governing authority and reap the benefits of His Kingdom lifestyle!

CULTURE OF
THE KINGDOM:
THE EPISTLES

When teaching about the "forest," sometimes I hear inquiries such as "Where is the Kingdom of God mentioned in the *Epistles*?" Or "Why didn't Paul teach about the Kingdom?" Actually, a close look at Paul's writings will readily reveal that, in most of his *Epistles*, he expended a lot of effort elaborating about the lifestyle required of Kingdom citizens. This obviously was a subject of great importance. In effect, Paul was instructing believers how to operate in the culture of the Kingdom of God. In *Acts 20:25-27*, Paul described his ministry, saying:

"And now, behold, I know that all of you, among whom I went about **preaching the kingdom** *[emphasis added], will no longer see my face. Therefore, I testify to you this day that I am innocent of the blood of all men. For I did not shrink from declaring to you the whole purpose of God."*

Also, *Acts 28:30-31* says about Paul,

"And he stayed two full years in his own rented quarters and was welcoming all who came to him, **preaching the Kingdom of God** *[emphasis added] and teaching concerning the Lord Jesus Christ with all openness, unhindered."*

Paul often preached about the Kingdom of God, expounding upon how to faithfully follow and serve Jesus Christ, the King. As would be expected, since Jesus continuously taught about His Kingdom, Paul spoke in depth about it as well. To teach about Jesus and what His disciples called "the Way," you must elaborate about His Kingdom.

From our earlier look at the first chapter of the *Book of Genesis*, we can recall how God originally gave Adam an assignment or a job to do, which was to exercise dominion. Later, Jesus came to the earth as the last Adam with a specific assignment from His Father, as well—to restore access to His Kingdom for humanity and to win back the dominion that Adam turned over to Satan. The Apostle Paul, as a Kingdom citizen, was also given a specific task from God. The primary purpose of his ministry was to bring the *Gospel* of the Kingdom to the Gentiles. His assignment was to reach non-Jewish people with the Good News about Christ and His Kingdom. He was called to preach the *Gospel* to them, telling them about the Kingdom, showing them how to become spiritually reborn, and then teaching those who received the gift of salvation how to live righteously. As a result of his great apostolic ministry and inspired *Epistles* to the churches, Paul is credited with penning two-thirds of the *New Testament*. In Acts 9:15, the Lord said to Ananias about Paul, *"Go, for he is a chosen instrument of Mine, to bear My name before the Gentiles and kings and the sons of Israel."* Then again, in *Acts 22:21*, Paul recalls the instructions from the Lord, who spoke to him on the road to Damascus, saying, *"Go! For I will send you far away to the Gentiles."*

Despite experiencing great personal suffering and numerous afflictions, the Apostle Paul remained dedicated to his unique assignment—travelling far and wide in order to bring the Kingdom message to the Gentile nations. Perhaps no other verse better defines Paul's call in relation to the Kingdom than does *Ephesians 6:19-20*, where he writes, *"... and pray on my behalf, that utterance may be given to me in the opening of my mouth, to make known with boldness the mystery of the Gospel, for which I am an ambassador in chains; that in proclaiming it I may speak boldly, as I ought to speak."*

Notice how Paul refers to himself as an "ambassador." This is not a religious term; however, it is a legal title for a government representative. Ambassador is defined by the **Oxford English Dictionary* as "... an accredited diplomat sent by a country as its official representative to a foreign nation." In the context of the "forest," Paul obviously considered himself to be a representative of the government of Christ's Kingdom. Paul was sent by the Lord as an emissary of His Kingdom to boldly proclaim the *Gospel*. What *Gospel* is that? The same *Gospel* that Jesus taught the disciples to preach, the *Gospel* of the coming Kingdom, whose doors have been opened to born-again, redeemed believers! Paul writes, *"Therefore, we are ambassadors for Christ, as though God were making an appeal through us; we beg you on behalf of Christ, be reconciled to God."* Here Paul indicates that all

---

*"Ambassador." Oxford English Dictionary. Oxford University Press, June 2021, www.oed.com. Accessed 15 June 2021.

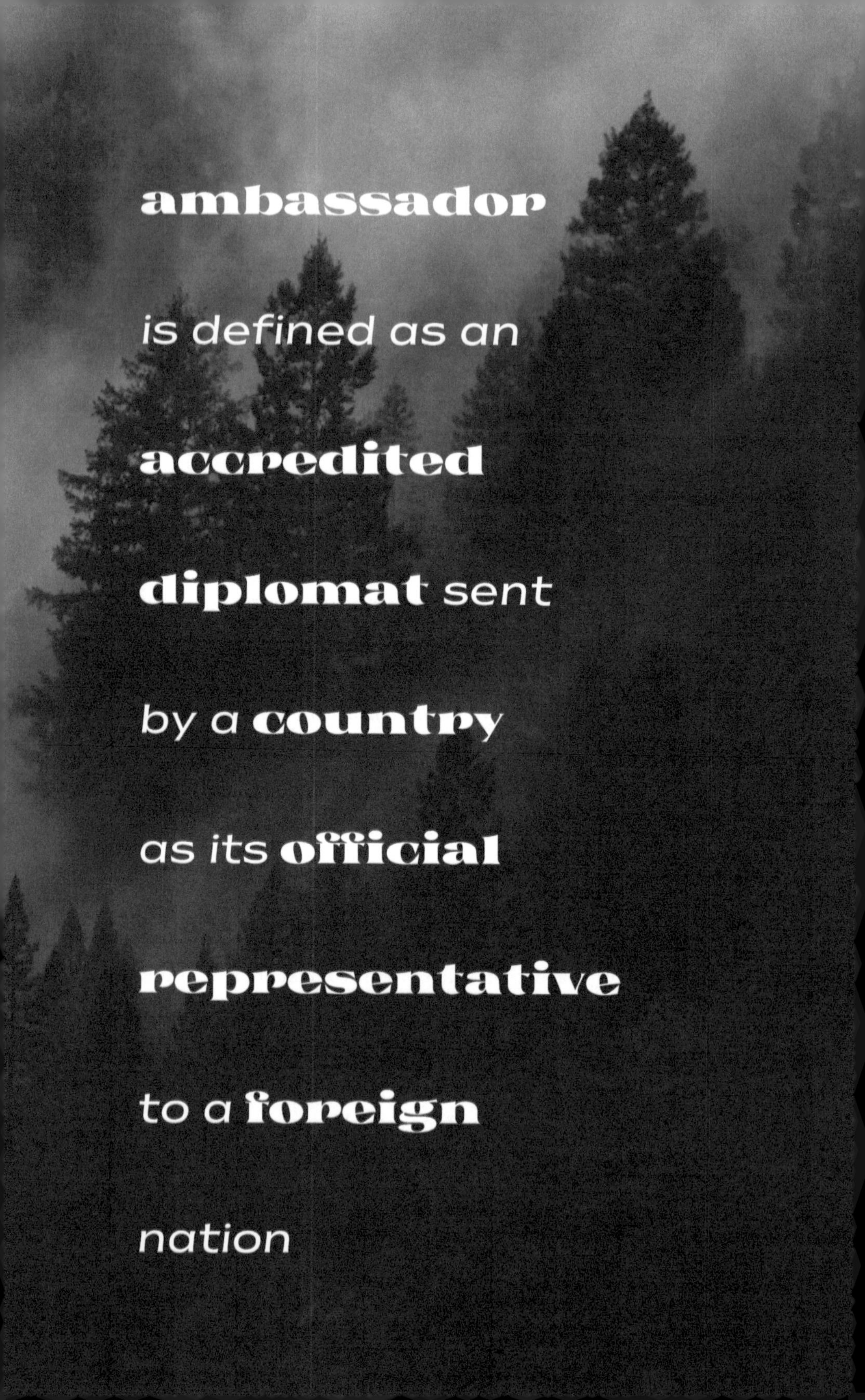

ambassador

is defined as an

accredited

diplomat sent

by a **country**

as its **official**

representative

to a **foreign**

nation

Kingdom citizens have been called to be ambassadors for God. This is our divine assignment. We are to represent the King to a lost and dying world, imploring all who remain outside the Kingdom to reconcile themselves to God. By doing so, as ambassadors of God's Kingdom, we are spreading the culture and rulership of Heaven to all of the earth.

As true ambassadors and representatives of Christ—our Lord and King—we must embrace His Kingdom lifestyle. "Well," you may be wondering, "What—exactly—is that lifestyle? And is there such a thing as a *Kingdom Ambassador's Training Manual?*" Well, those are good things to think about. Paul's many letters to the churches supply good instructions for righteous living and focus on proper conduct of a good ambassador of the Kingdom. He provides numerous descriptions, instructions, and corrections relating to Godly living and ambassadorship. For example, in a letter written to the Ephesians, Paul says, *"Therefore I, the prisoner of the Lord, implore you to walk in a manner worthy of the calling with which you have been called, with all humility and gentleness, with patience, showing tolerance for one another in love, being diligent to preserve the unity of the Spirit in the bond of peace"* (*Ephesians 4:1*). Here, he is giving encouragement and instruction to the church on how we, as spirit-filled believers, should operate in our daily lives. Paul is delineating proper conduct of ambassadors of the Kingdom.

In *Philippians 4:4-7*, Paul writes,

> *"Rejoice in the Lord always; again I will say, rejoice! Let your gentle spirit be known to all men. The Lord is near. Be anxious for nothing, but in everything by prayer and supplication with thanksgiving let your requests be made known to God. And the peace of God, which surpasses all comprehension, will guard your hearts and your minds in Christ Jesus."*

Paul is instructing the church, all who follow Christ as Lord, not to worry about anything but to simply trust in the Lord to provide. In essence, he is saying that "everything you need will be provided for you if you just ask the King with faith and do not doubt Him!" Praise God! In fact, the *Scriptures* tell us to be joyful in all circumstances. *James 1:2 (NKJV)* says, "*My brethren, count it all joy when you fall into various trials ...*" And again, in *Thessalonians 5:16-18 (NKJV)*, Paul proclaims, "*Rejoice always, pray without ceasing, in everything give thanks; for this is the will of God in Christ Jesus for you.*" As citizens and ambassadors connected to His royal realm, we can rejoice in the Lord always! This reflects our joyous Kingdom lifestyle.

Although Paul wrote most of the *New Testament*, he was certainly not the only author who taught the Kingdom's culture to the churches. Peter was, as we know from the *Gospels*, a disciple who daily walked with Jesus for three years. We can be certain that Peter knew a great deal about the Kingdom of God, because he listened to his Lord, Jesus, talking about His Kingdom daily. In *1 Peter 2:9*, Peter quotes the *Old Testament*, "*But you are a chosen race, a royal priesthood, a Holy Nation, a people for God's own possession ...*" Peter is emphasizing to the church that we belong to a Kingdom owned by God. We are His people set apart to Him. *1 Peter 2:9* goes on to point out that it is our duty to "*... proclaim the excellencies of Him who called us out of darkness into His marvelous light.*"

Peter addresses the church in *1 Peter 2:1-3,*

"Therefore, putting aside all malice and all deceit and hypocrisy and envy and all slander, like newborn babies, long for the pure milk of the word, so that by it you may grow in respect to salvation, if you have tasted the kindness of the Lord."

Here, he is instructing that believers are to stop the evil practices of malice, deceit, hypocrisy, and slander; instead, they are to crave the *Word of God* so that they can grow into mature citizens of the Kingdom. He is explaining the Kingdom principle of growing up spiritually, which is based upon maturing through the daily consumption of the *Word of God* in order to live a life in keeping with the culture of God. Our lives should emulate the Kingdom culture as we learn more and more by becoming grounded in *His Word* in its full context through the guidance and anointing of the Holy Spirit.

There is so much instruction for Godly living found in the *New Testament* that we cannot begin to discuss it all at once. I encourage you to prayerfully study the *New Testament* in its full context, thereby learning the culture of the Kingdom from the very Source—the entire *Word of God*—the "forest." Meanwhile, I have highlighted below a few more examples of *New Testament* scriptures useful for instruction about Kingdom living. Remember, as you read these and other *Scriptures*, keep in mind the concept of the whole "forest."

> *Ephesians 4:17-24: "So this I say, and affirm together with the Lord, that you walk no longer just as the Gentiles also walk, in the futility of their mind, being darkened in their understanding, excluded from the life of God because of the ignorance that is in them, because of the hardness of their heart; and they, having become callous, have given themselves over to sensuality for the practice of every kind of impurity with greediness. But you did not learn Christ in this way, if indeed you have heard Him and have been taught in Him, just as truth is in Jesus, that, in reference to your former manner of life, you lay aside the old self, which is being corrupted in accordance with the lusts of deceit, and that you be renewed in the spirit of your mind, and put on*

the new self, which in the likeness of God has been created in righteousness and holiness of the truth."

Ephesians 5:1-5: "Therefore be imitators of God, as beloved children; and walk in love, just as Christ also loved you and gave Himself up for us, an offering and a sacrifice to God as a fragrant aroma. But immorality or any impurity or greed must not even be named among you, as is proper among saints; and there must be no filthiness and silly talk, or coarse jesting, which are not fitting, but rather giving of thanks. For this you know with certainty, that no immoral or impure person or covetous man, who is an idolater, has an inheritance in the kingdom of Christ and God."

2 Timothy 4:1-5: "I solemnly charge you in the presence of God and of Christ Jesus, who is to judge the living and the dead, and by His appearing and His kingdom: preach the word; be ready in season and out of season; reprove, rebuke, exhort, with great patience and instruction. For the time will come when they will not endure sound doctrine; but wanting to have their ears tickled, they will accumulate for themselves teachers in accordance to their own desires, and will turn away their ears from the truth and will turn aside to myths. But you, be sober in all things, endure hardship, do the work of an evangelist, fulfill your ministry."

James 2:1-5: "My brethren, do not hold your faith in our glorious Lord Jesus Christ with an attitude of personal favoritism. For if a man comes into your assembly with a gold ring and dressed in fine clothes, and there also comes in a poor man in dirty clothes, and you pay special attention to the one who is wearing the fine clothes, and say, 'You sit here in a good place,' and you say to the poor man, "You stand over there, or sit down by my footstool," have you not made distinctions among yourselves, and become judges with evil motives? Listen, my beloved brethren: did not God choose the poor of this world to be rich in faith and heirs of the kingdom which He promised to those who love Him?"

1 Peter 1:13-16: "Therefore, prepare your minds for action, keep sober in spirit, fix your hope completely on the grace to be brought to you at the revelation of Jesus Christ. As obedient children, do not be conformed to the former lusts which were yours in your ignorance, but like the Holy One who called you, be holy yourselves also in all your behavior; because it is written, 'YOU SHALL BE HOLY, FOR I AM HOLY.'"

2 Peter 1:4-11: "For by these He has granted to us His precious and magnificent promises, so that by them you may become partakers of the divine nature, having escaped the corruption that is in the world by lust. Now for this very reason also, applying all diligence, in your faith supply moral excellence, and in your moral excellence, knowledge, and in your knowledge, self-control, and in your self-control, perseverance, and in your perseverance, godliness, and in your godliness, brotherly kindness, and in your brotherly kindness, love. For if these qualities are yours and are increasing, they render you neither useless nor unfruitful in the true knowledge of our Lord Jesus Christ. For he who lacks these qualities is blind or short-sighted, having forgotten his purification from his former sins. Therefore, brethren, be all the more diligent to make certain about His calling and choosing you; for as long as you practice these things, you will never stumble; for in this way the entrance into the eternal kingdom of our Lord and Savior Jesus Christ will be abundantly supplied to you."

God speaks to us through His anointed authors who penned the *New Testament*, giving guidelines and wisdom for how to operate in dominion and Godliness. In essence, these Spirit-inspired words expound upon the culture and nature of God Himself, explained in such a way that we can apply them to our daily lives. God gave us these anointed writings to help mature us in our faith walk and to provide us with instructions how to operate as ambassadors of the King! We need to prayerfully study them under the guidance of the Holy Spirit, so that we can learn how to live the Kingdom lifestyle. Again, this short list of Kingdom teachings, applied in full context, represents advice and instruction for righteous living. Adam lost his righteousness, but—through Christ, our Savior and Redeemer—those who repent and make Him Lord have regained what Adam lost! By renewing our minds, guarding our hearts, and submitting to the guidance of the Holy Spirit, we can live righteously before the King! That is how we are to live now, since we are in the Kingdom of God and outside of the kingdom of darkness!

WHAT ABOUT THE TREES?

Now that we have seen the "forest" of the Word, with a full focus on God's unfolding plan to bring His Kingdom to the earth, let us talk about the "trees." Since you cannot have a forest without trees, the "forest" of the *Bible* is obviously made up of many "trees." Each "tree" should be fully valued in context with all of *God's Word*. In no part of this book will you find it implied that the worth of any of the "trees of the forest" should be diminished. Rather, our premise is simply that each "tree" should only be considered in the context of the "forest" as a whole. So, we are not doing away with, nor depreciating, any truth from the *Word of God*. Conversely, we are rediscovering each truth through the correct lens of the Kingdom.

For example, let us consider the subject of "divine healing" applied in the context of the Kingdom. I mean—since the healing of our physical bodies is such an excellent benefit of being a Kingdom citizen—how could we not talk about it? *Matthew 8:17* says, *"This was to fulfill what was spoken through Isaiah the prophet: 'He Himself took our infirmities and carried away our diseases.'"* What a huge blessing it is that we have a loving Father in Heaven who wants His children healthy and free of any illness or infirmity! When considering the whole "forest," the "tree" of "healing" is just one of many parts of the Kingdom. Specifically, the covenant of healing for our bodies is actually the Kingdom government's healthcare system. Think about it. Many nations today provide a healthcare system for their citizens; so does the Government of God make provision for its citizens' health. Let me emphatically boast that the Kingdom's healthcare plan is far better than any healthcare system that man ever devised. The same God who formed our bodies in the beginning surely knows best how to heal our bodies today. He is, after all, "Jehovah Rapha, the Lord who heals us!" Glory!

Never forget that everything and everyone in a Kingdom belongs to the King Himself. The King exercises full ownership over all of His citizens—who are his children. Since a king measures his wealth by what belongs to him, it makes perfect sense that our King desires us to be free of sickness and disease. When we are healthy and whole, it shows the lost world that we serve a good King who takes great care of us. *John 10* calls Jesus *"the good shepherd"* and our Good Shepherd always desires to see His flock in good physical condition. That is why Jesus went about preaching the Kingdom of God, doing good and healing all who were sick. When we walk in divine health, it gives glory and honor to our King. It shows that He truly is the Good Shepherd. It is now—and always has been—the Lord's will to heal us and for us to walk in faith that He will.

Again, just as some large companies offer great healthcare benefits to their employees, our King offers complete healing for all citizens of His Kingdom. Jesus finished the work of healing by sacrificing His body to be broken during His crucifixion. 1 Peter 2:24 states, " ... and He Himself bore our sins in His body on the cross, so that we might die to sin and live to righteousness; for by His wounds you were healed." The past tense, "were," here, tells us that Jesus already paid the price for healing! We must now receive that healing "by faith" in *His Word*. For in the Kingdom, the only currency needed for healing is faith. On numerous occasions in the four *Gospels*, Jesus informed people whom he healed that it was through their faith that they were made whole. We must receive healing not as "a separate truth" of the Word but for what it is, a benefit of the Kingdom!

There are many exciting truths ("trees") in God's Kingdom. *Psalms 103:1-2* says, *"Bless the Lord, O my soul, and all that is within me, bless His holy name. Bless the Lord, O my soul, and forget none of His benefits."* Let us briefly list a few of these beneficial "trees" found in His Kingdom:

Kingdom Provision:

> *Psalms 37:25-26 (NIV) "I was young and now I am old, yet I have never seen the righteous forsaken or their children begging bread. They are always generous and lend freely; their children will be blessed."*

we are **not doing away** with any **truth** from the Word of God but instead **rediscovering** the **truth** through the correct context of the **Kingdom** of **God**

Philippians 4:19 (NLT) "And this same God who takes care of me will supply [fill to the full] all your needs from his glorious riches, which have been given to us in Christ Jesus."

Kingdom Education:

John 14:25-26 (NLT) "I am telling you these things now while I am still with you. But when the Father sends the Advocate as my representative–that is, the Holy Spirit–he will teach you everything and will remind you of everything I have told you."

Kingdom Keys:

Matthew 16:19 "I will give you the keys of the kingdom of heaven; and whatever you bind on earth shall have been bound in heaven, and whatever you loose on earth shall have been loosed in heaven."

Isaiah 22:22 "Then I will set the key of the house of David on his shoulder, When he opens no one will shut, When he shuts no one will open."

Kingdom Economics:

Luke 6:38 (AMP) "Give, and [gifts] will be given to you; good measure, pressed down, shaken together, and running over, will they pour into [the pouch formed by] the bosom [of your robe and used as a bag]. For with the measure you deal out [with the measure you use when you confer benefits on others], it will be measured back to you."

Luke 18:22 (AMP) "And when Jesus heard it, He said to him, 'One thing you still lack. Sell everything that you have and divide [the money] among the poor, and you will have [rich] treasure in heaven; and come back [and] follow Me [become My disciple, join My party, and accompany Me].'"

Kingdom Delegated Authority:

John 20:21-22 "So Jesus said to them again, 'Peace be with you; as the Father has sent Me, I also send you.' And when He had said this, He breathed on them and said to them, "Receive the Holy Spirit."

Matthew 28:18-20 "And Jesus came up and spoke to them, saying, 'All authority has   been given to Me in heaven and on earth. Go therefore and make disciples of all the nations, baptizing them in the name of the Father and the Son and the Holy Spirit, teaching them to observe all that I   commanded you; and lo, I am with you always, even to the end of the age.'"

THE TREE OF SALVATION

In the introduction of this book, we briefly focused on one of the "trees" in the "forest"—truth about the subject of "Salvation." As previously stated, I consider what the *Bible* teaches about salvation to be one of the more wonderful and amazing Biblical truths. One of my favorite *Scriptures* is *Romans 10:9*, where it says, "... *that if you confess with your mouth Jesus as Lord, and believe in your heart that God raised Him from the dead, you will be saved.*" It is a privilege to share the message of salvation. In fact, nothing is more exciting than seeing people respond to the call to surrender their lives to Christ and enter the Kingdom of God. Nothing produces more joy than witnessing someone becoming born again by repenting and making Jesus Christ their Lord. *Luke 15:10 (NKJV)* proclaims, *"... there is joy in the presence of angels over one sinner who repents."* Even the angels celebrate when someone gets saved! Sharing the message of salvation is something I love to do. However, in cases where preachers and churches focus intently on salvation and little else, the message of what it means to be born again gets shrunk into something that loses power—like plugging something into a power outlet and then pulling the plug. The truth of salvation needs to be applied to the full context of *God's Word.* Salvation opens the door for transformation to a new and better life, here and now, as a citizen in God's Kingdom, and the new believer needs to be connected to all that the Kingdom lifestyle entails.

We know from our present study that Jesus daily preached and taught about the Kingdom of God, but only once in all of the *Gospel* accounts of His life does He actually mention being "born again" and, even then, He immediately relates being "born again" to the Kingdom of God. The *Gospel* of John gives an account of Jesus being approached by a man named Nicodemus in the middle of the night. *John 3:1-3* states,

> *"Now there was a man of the Pharisees, named Nicodemus, a ruler of the Jews; this man came to Jesus by night and said to Him, 'Rabbi, we know that You have come from God as a teacher; for no one can do these signs that You do unless God is with him.' Jesus answered and said to him, "Truly, truly, I say to you, unless one is born again he cannot see the Kingdom of God."*

This account is not about a public moment in Jesus' life; rather, it is about Jesus responding during a private conversation. Jesus is saying that "to see the Kingdom of God" one must be "reborn" from above. That is actually how a person enters into the Kingdom of God. Let me emphasize that becoming "born again" is the beginning, or the entrance, not the destination, itself. The fact that Jesus uses the phrase "born again" is significant, because citizenship in the Kingdom is all about birthright. A person cannot purchase entrance into the Kingdom of God. Neither can anyone, just by being "a good enough person," earn or claim a place in His Kingdom. No! There is only one way to enter the Kingdom of God. We **must** first be spiritually "born again"—born from above—which gives us the legal birthright to be called "children of God" and "citizens of His Kingdom."

Remember that God's Kingdom is made up of The King and His royal offspring. *Revelation 19:16* proclaims Jesus to be the "King of kings." The word "kings" in the phrase "King of kings"actually refers to born-again citizens of the Kingdom. It is the title of all for whom "the King" has re-established dominion. *Romans 5:7 (NKJV)* says,

> *"For if by the one man's offense [Adam's] death reigned through the one, much more those who receive abundance of grace and the gift of righteousness [right standing] will reign in life through the One, Jesus Christ."*

He is "the King;" yes, He is! But we are considered "kings," ourselves, within His Kingdom, and we reign with Him with authority to exercise dominion. Glory! The Kingdom of God is the only Kingdom ever to exist where all its citizens are also royalty! That is the significance of being born again. It gives us the right to enter God's royal bloodline and to "reign" with Christ. The Apostle Paul says, in *Romans 5:17*,

> *"For if by the transgression of the one, death reigned through the one, much more those who receive the abundance of grace*

and of the gift of righteousness will reign in life through the One, Jesus Christ."

Many churches today focus so intently on the salvation message that they misguidedly treat the "prayer of salvation" as if it, alone, were the only thing that really matters to God. It is as if receiving the gift of salvation were the one true goal in life, only because it provides assurance that one day we will go to Heaven. Receiving the gift of salvation is often presented as the way to "escape the torments of hell" by obtaining "a free ticket" or "a pass" to get to Heaven down the road just by saying a prayer. Kind of like accepting a free ticket just so you will be ready for the train when it comes to pick you up. Just hang on to your ticket and you are in great shape. The ticket is to believe in Jesus as your Savior, without much being spoken about truly making Him Lord. This is, indeed, a limited view of what salvation means. To transition to Heaven from our earthly life, we must receive the gift of salvation by the grace of God, but true repentance and becoming born again provide us with the keys to God's Kingdom, so we can enter, right now, as citizens "fired up" about fulfilling the King's purpose for our everyday lives. We accept the gift of Salvation through grace so we can become what Jesus called "fruitful." To be fruitful citizens of the Kingdom, we must be productive. Being a citizen of the Kingdom is not about sitting on the bench waiting for the train to arrive.

When looking at the entire "forest," we understand that salvation is really about the doors of the Kingdom being opened so that, as born-again believers—through the power of the Holy Spirit and the building of our faith through the hearing and study of the *Word of God* in its full context—we will be able to help bring Heaven's culture to this earth. Getting saved is less about getting ready to leave the earth and more about getting ready to reach out to the world to advance God's Kingdom here and now. Hallelujah! There is nothing the **Kingdom** of **God** is the **only** **Kingdom** ever to exist where its **citizens** are also **royalty** more secure than being an active citizen in God's Kingdom right now, and you do not have to wait to get there.

Sadly, too many times in the church, people have entered the Kingdom through salvation but have failed to continue on the path to spiritual maturity. When someone gets "saved" but does not become "discipled" in the Kingdom culture, it is just like taking a newborn baby and placing the infant somewhere alone to fend for itself. We are talking about "easy pickings" for the enemy, who hates to see anyone grow in their faith walk. *1 Peter 2:1-3* urges all new-born believers to "*... desire the sincere milk of the Word, that you may grow thereby.*"

God desires for us to enter into the Kingdom, then to grow up spiritually to a point of maturity so that we can fulfill His purpose for our lives. To grow into spiritual maturity requires that we learn through prayerful daily study of the *Bible*, as we progress through all of the *Scriptures*. We also need to be taught from all of the counsel of the *Bible*—not just the one truth of salvation. Show me a person who gets saved but learns little more from the *Scriptures*, and I will show you a spiritual baby with improper covering. We must diligently study the Word in its full context through the guidance of the Holy Spirit, in order to grow by it. *Romans 10:17 (NKJV)* says,

> "*So then faith comes by hearing, and hearing by the Word of God.*"

Growing in the faith by learning from *God's Word* is absolutely essential to spiritual maturity and a Kingdom citizen should never stop growing. And the journey of spiritual growth involves exploring all the "trees" of the "forest," not just a select few.

Jesus' great commission was not to go into the world to preach salvation only. No. He said specifically, in *Matthew 28:19 (NKJV)*, "*Go therefore and make disciples of all the nations.*" The command to "make disciples" infers continuous training beyond initial salvation from sin. A born-again believer needs to learn by example and through instruction, in order to grow strong in the faith. When the message of salvation is watered down to just a simple prayer of confession, it becomes just a religious "tree." The full salvation message must be connected to Kingdom living. In fact, true repentance requires an individual to make Jesus Christ the Lord of all aspects of life, submitting daily to the leadership of the Holy Spirit. Jesus must become the Lord, literally, "supreme in authority," in order for a person to become transformed into a true Kingdom citizen.

It is logical and straightforward. If you want to enjoy the benefits of Kingdom citizenship, then the King must be your Lord. You must ask Him to forgive all of your sins, repenting by making Him the Lord of every aspect of your life, becoming baptised, and seeking and submitting to the guidance of the Holy Spirit. Each day, you must consistently place Him first in your life. That is how you become born again into His Kingdom and embrace the Kingdom lifestyle. This is why Jesus repeatedly taught about the Kingdom, so that people would listen and ask Him how to enter into His Kingdom. This created a desire within people who listened to Him to have what He had, and then He would explain the method of entry. Salvation is the doorway by which people enter into the Kingdom. It is the first "tree" they must pass as they enter the "forest." Focusing on salvation as a prayer of confession, alone—without applying it to the full context of the Word, including an actual understanding of the Lordship/Kingship of Jesus and what it means to really surrender your life to Christ—is not seeing the whole "forest." That limited view leaves far too much on the table. When we are born again, we take on a new life in Christ. When we fully submit our lives to the King, He will transform us into what the Apostle Paul termed "a new creature in Christ." He will shape those who make Him Lord, changing each one into the person He intended for them to be, so they can reign with Him!

Perhaps you are reading this and thinking, "Pastor Earl. I've never made Jesus Christ my Lord and savior," or "All this Kingdom of God stuff sounds awesome. I really want in on it!" Or maybe you once prayed the prayer of salvation, after deciding to make Jesus Lord, but you now realize that you need to live up to His Kingdom standards. Either way, are you now ready to enter and to operate in the greatest Kingdom the planet has ever known? Are you willing to set aside your own will and desires, allowing Jesus Christ to have full Lordship over your life? If you are ready to live with real purpose and to fulfill your true destiny, then you can decide right now to accept all that the Kingdom offers! *John 3:16-17* says,

> *"For God so loved the world, that He gave His only begotten Son, that whoever believes in Him shall not perish, but have eternal life. For God did not send the Son into the world to judge the world, but that the world might be saved through Him."*

God sent His Son, Jesus Christ, into the earth to reclaim humanity's right to enter into the Kingdom of God. If you are ready to believe the *Word of God* and to be part of His Kingdom—then pray this prayer with your mouth, believing it in your heart:

Dear Heavenly Father,

I come to you in the name of Jesus Christ, Your Son. It says in Your Holy Word that "Whoever will call on the name of the Lord will be saved (Romans 10:13)." I'm now calling on your name, so I know You have saved me from my sins, and you have brought me into Your kingdom.

In Romans 10:9-10, You also said "... if you confess with your mouth Jesus as Lord, and believe in your heart that God raised Him from the dead, you will be saved; for with the heart a person believes, resulting in righteousness, and with the mouth he confesses, resulting in salvation." I do believe in my heart now that Jesus Christ is the Son of God. I believe that He was raised from the dead for my justification and I confess Him now as my Lord.

Lord, because Your Word says, in John 3:3, "Truly, truly, I say to you, unless one is born again he cannot see the Kingdom of God," I do believe that I am now a citizen of the Kingdom of God. Like it says in 2 Corinthians 5:21, "I have become the righteousness of God in Christ Jesus." Thank you, Lord, I am saved and ready to live for You, my King. Amen!

If you just prayed the above prayer and truly meant it with all your heart, then you are now part of the Kingdom of God! Hallelujah!

Now it is very important that you begin reading the *Bible*, studying *God's Word* so that your mind can be renewed. As mentioned earlier, Romans 12:2 tells us, *"And do not be conformed to this world, but be transformed by the renewing of your mind, so that you may prove what the will of God is, that which is good, and acceptable, and perfect."*

As we previously pointed out, it is so very important as Kingdom citizens that we become diligent students of the *Word of God*. That is how we grow and learn about who we are in Christ. Think of the *Scriptures* the same way you think about food. At meal time you get hungry and you eat so you will stay strong. Most of us are not in the habit of skipping meals, unless we have a reason for fasting. To grow and to become strong as a born-again citizen in God's Kingdom, you need a steady diet of feasting on *God's Word*. It is also important that you find and become connected with a solid church where you can develop personal relationships with mature believers who can help support you as you grow mature in Christ. Becoming part of a church body will open up opportunities for interpersonal relationships, training, and opportunities to serve by spreading the Kingdom *Gospel* and helping grow God's Kingdom in and on the earth. Pray and ask God to show you the right church that He would have you join as you begin to seek the Kingdom of God. I promise that He will reveal Himself to you. Being faithful to a good, *Bible*-believing church is a necessity for successful Kingdom living, and it will help you in your faith walk as you seek to grow mature in Christ.

THE FINAL WORD

Throughout this book, we have endeavored to interpret the *Bible* in its original context—which is the Kingdom of God. Looking through the lens of the Kingdom provides a clear perspective of who our Creator is, what His original intentions were for this earth, and how His plans for His creation have not changed. His Kingdom government and His plans to establish His Kingdom, in and on the earth, are what ties all of the *Scriptures* together. His Kingdom is "the forest" of which we must never lose sight. Here are a few important points to consider as you study all of *God's Word*:

1. If Adam had never eaten the forbidden fruit, where would he be today?

2. God created Adam as a son and gave him all dominion over the planet.

3. Adam did not fall from Heaven; he fell from his position of dominion.

4. Adam did not lose a religion; he lost his personal relationship with his Creator and access to the Kingdom of God.

5. Jesus restored access to the Kingdom of God for humanity—for all who believe and make Him Lord.

6. Every miracle Jesus performed was done by exercising His dominion over the planet.

7. The *Bible* is not about a religion or religions; it is about a King, His Kingdom, and His royal offspring.

Remember that, from reading the *Bible* in its full context, we learn that, as born-again believers and followers of Christ, we are royal citizens of a Kingdom ruled by a benevolent God who loves us and with whom we can have a personal relationship. Wow! What a marvelous concept! God created man as a son and gave him dominion over all the earth. Although man fell and lost access to the Kingdom, God, Who is loving, graceful, and willing to forgive, already had a plan to restore humankind by sending His seed as our Redeemer. Jesus Christ restored the Kingdom for humanity and—through His death, burial, and resurrection—we are now able to regain what the first Adam relinquished! Praise God!

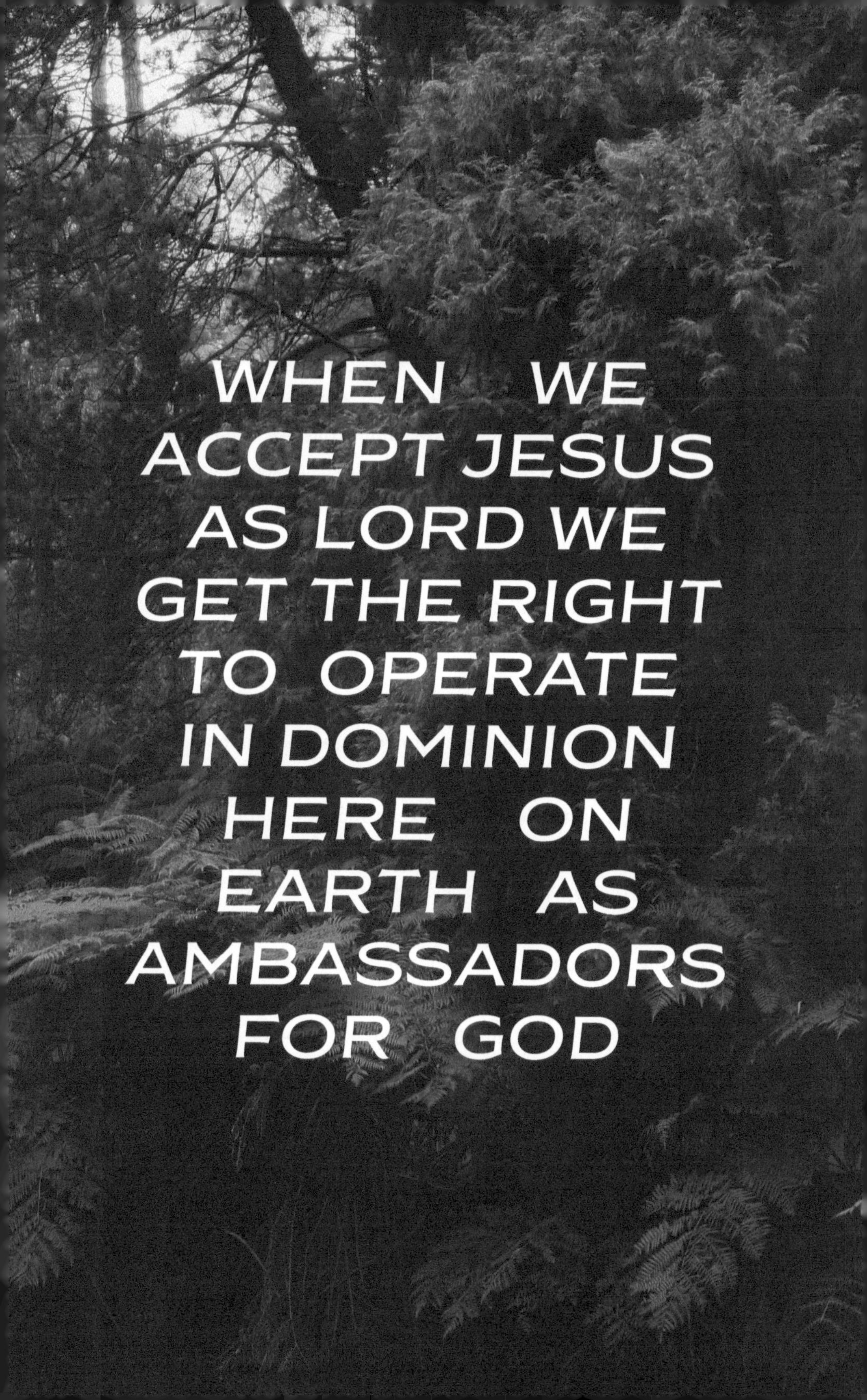

WHEN WE
ACCEPT JESUS
AS LORD WE
GET THE RIGHT
TO OPERATE
IN DOMINION
HERE ON
EARTH AS
AMBASSADORS
FOR GOD

Jesus said to His disciples, in *Matthew 24:14*,

"This Gospel of the kingdom shall be preached in the whole world as a testimony to all the nations, and then the end will come."

By this, we understand that, as disciples and ambassadors of Christ, our chief assignment is to go about proclaiming the GOOD NEWS OF THE KINGDOM! When the Holy Spirit guides us to speak, we must never be shy or embarrassed to share His *Gospel* message. In *Romans 1:16* (NIV), Paul proclaims,

"For I am not ashamed of the Gospel, because it is the power of God that brings salvation to everyone who believes; first to the Jew, then to the Gentile."

We must remember to daily embrace our collective assignment as the children of God to proclaim that the Kingdom is here—through what we say and how we act! Although everyone and every nation may not accept the invitation into God's Kingdom, as His ambassadors, we must give them the opportunity to hear about it and to see the Kingdom lifestyle by how we live. That is why everything that I preach is in the context of the Kingdom. Let us endeavor to be consumed with the Kingdom, just like Jesus was when He walked the earth. Our Lord wants us to help spread His Kingdom, not to help promote a religion.

When we accept Jesus as Lord, we are afforded the right and power through faith to operate in dominion, here and now, as ambassadors for God on the earth. In *John 14:12* (NIV), Jesus said,

"Very truly I tell you, whoever believes in me will do the works I have been doing, and they will do even greater things than these, because I am going to the Father."

Realizing the full truth of *God's Word*, of who we are in Christ, of what it means to be a citizen of His Kingdom, will fill us with inspiration to serve our King with great vigor and expectation—keeping our hearts pure and contrite. As ambassadors of Christ, we must walk in faith and righteousness, boldly representing the Kingdom. In *Romans 10:17*, the great ambassador for Christ, the Apostle Paul, says, *"So faith comes from hearing, and hearing by the word of Christ."* Indeed, our faith and ability to live righteously are strengthened through knowledge of *God's Word*, as we make sure to never lose sight of the "forest."

Rather than focusing on just a few aspects of God's truth and devoting all of our time and attention to that, as disciples of Christ, let us attempt to grasp as much of *God's Word* as possible—applying what we learn to the full context of the *Bible*. With the proper Kingdom lens and focus, we can study the Word through the correct context that God intended. It is in no manner edifying to become burdened down with the "baggage" of out-of-context religious thinking. Only when we take into account the entire "forest," can we fully value and understand all of the "trees" found in it. It is "by seeking first the Kingdom" that we will ultimately fulfill our destiny, by proclaiming the full *Gospel* to the world. Remember what Jesus promised in *Matthew 6:33* (NKJV), *"But seek first the Kingdom of God and His righteousness, and all these things shall be added to you."*

Never let it be said that you "failed to see the forest for the trees." Live the Kingdom lifestyle! Amen!

ABOUT THE AUTHOR

Born and raised in the Gainesville area of north-central Florida, Pastor Earl's call to ministry in 1993 proved to be a significant marker in his life. One morning, while praying on his way to work in Atlanta, Georgia, he experienced a vision. Suddenly, the windshield of his truck displayed a gathering of thousands of people, and he saw himself standing before them preaching. This confirmed God's call to ministry on his life. Since answering the call, Pastor Earl has worked in nearly every facet of ministry: children, youth, young adults. In 2004, he and his wife, Marci, launched Anchor Faith Church, in St. Augustine, Florida, where they continue to serve as senior pastors. Both are alumni of Rhema *Bible* Training College, having graduated in 2000. Pastor Earl presently serves as Regional Director for Rhema Ministerial Association International. He loves living in St. Augustine, Florida and spending quality time with his wife, children and grandchildren.

The Vision of Anchor Faith Church is to "ignite the city, impact the nation and influence the world," helping the Lord build His Kingdom in and on the earth. Toward this goal, through its Kingdom Institute, the church provides, at convenient times, an extensive curriculum for new believers and anyone interested in increasing their knowledge and understanding of Biblical Truth.

Pastor Earl encourages the church body to become involved in ministry outreach in the community and beyond. There are opportunities to participate on many levels, with classes provided to help prepare vision partners to reach out in areas where God has gifted them to serve.

Anchor Faith has a strong youth ministry. The church cares deeply about providing for the well-being of children and young adults. As one of its more important areas of ministry, Anchor Faith

operates a private Christian school, providing quality education in a wholesome environment.

Anchor Faith is also greatly committed to world outreach, as the church supports numerous ministries around the earth. Always glad for opportunities to spread the message of "Kingdom Living," Pastor Earl has accepted invitations to visit and to teach at churches in many nations and nationally and locally as well. Through Pastor Earl's leadership, Anchor Faith has planted churches in Valdosta, Georgia and Managua, Nicaragua. Additionally, the church fully supports an orphanage in New Delhi, India.

Find Pastor Earl Glisson around the web at:
@earlglisson & fb.com/earlwglisson

I would like to thank the following people, without whose help, this book would not have been possible:

Daniel Melton

John Greene

Mearys Greene

Amita Lahiri

Anila Lahiri

Bryan Adkins

Stormi Harrington Willis

Todd Fooshée

Rod Gillmore

If you would like more information about Pastor Earl Glisson, additional kingdom teaching, or would like to find out more about their work in St. Augustine, Florida, please visit Anchor Faith Church on the web.

Anchor Faith Library

Other books by **Pastor Earl Glisson**

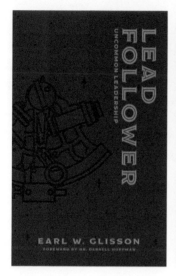
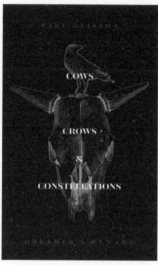

Books from our other authors

Visit anchorfaith.store for more information
and to order one of these great resources.

KINGDOM

Book design & cover illustration by
Todd Fooshée

You can find more of his work at
dribbble.com/toddfooshee